THE BLACK AT PLAY

ALTON DOUGLAS
DENNIS MOORE
ADDITIONAL RESEARCH BY JO DOUGLAS

New Year's Eve Dance, Gala Baths, West Bromwich, 1957.

©1994 ALTON and JO DOUGLAS, DENNIS MOORE
ISBN 0 947865 08 X

Published by Beacon Broadcasting Ltd., 267 Tettenhall Road, Wolverhampton WV6 0DQ.
Printed by Windmill Printing, Oldbury Road, West Bromwich, West Midlands. B70 9DQ.

Layout by Alton and Jo Douglas.

Kingswinford Gala, 13th June 1959.

Front cover: Brierley Hill Carnival, 1958.

CONTENTS

THE BLACK COUNTRY MUSEUM

It's a great family day out

Tipton Road, Dudley. Only 3 miles from Junction 2 M5. Tel: 021-552 9643

YA 36426

The Black Country Museum-Tramway

OUT	EXCHANGE	IN
Depot	Colliery	Village	This ticket must be punched in the stage to which the Passenger is entitled to travel and shown on demand. Issued subject to Museum Regulations. Travel at risk of passenger. Not transferable	Depot	Colliery	Village
or Dog	Luggage			Luggage	or Dog

Bell Punch Co., Ltd., London

COME BACK BY TRAM

FARE ADULT 10p
CHILD/O.A.P. 5p

ALLOWS STOP AT COLLIERY

The Duke of Gloucester officially opens the school at the Black Country Museum, 12th May 1992. Pupils of the Jesson C. of E. School, Dudley, take a step back in time for the occasion.

The inaugural trip on a restored tram, Black Country Museum, August 1980.

A school party escorted around the site by a member of The Black Country Museum staff, 1987.

Reg Bennett acts the part, as he dispenses medicines in Emile Doo's reconstructed chemist shop, at the Black Country Museum, 1982. The shop, its contents and frontage, had been transported from its original site in Halesowen Road, Netherton.

IN THE BEGINNING

Wrens Nest, Dudley, c. 1900.

The Paddling Pool, Dartmouth Park, West Bromwich, c. 1918.

Silver Jubilee Park, Coseley, 1936.

Wolverhampton Municipal Secondary School Football Team, 1939/40.

6

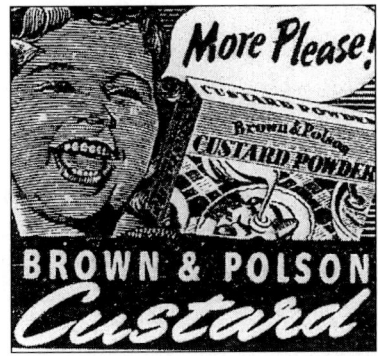

ROWNTREE'S
PERSONAL POINTS VALUES

1945

Owing to Zoning, the distribution of Rowntree's Chocolate and Clear Gums is now limited to certain parts of the country, mainly in the North and East. We are optimistic enough to hope that our products will soon be available again everywhere.

✱

This is the second week of Ration Period No. 11.

ROWNTREE'S BLENDED CHOCOLATE

3d. (2 points)

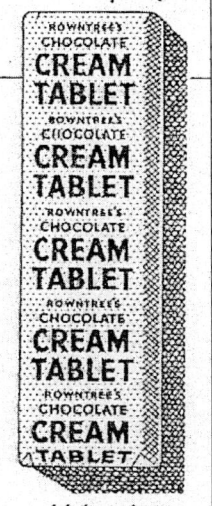

ROWNTREE'S CHOCOLATE CREAM TABLET

2½d. (2 points)

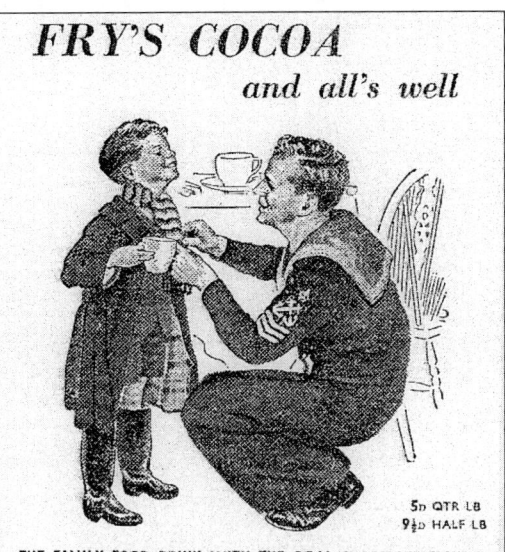
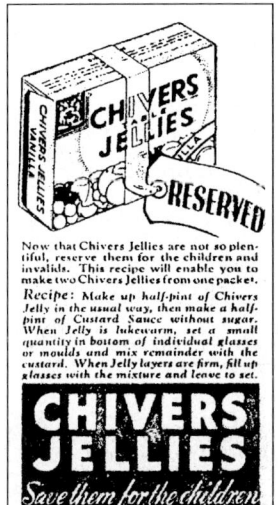

FOOD FACTS
CHRISTMAS FANCIES

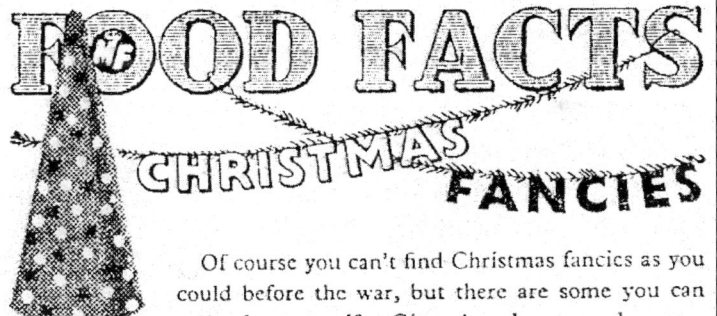

Of course you can't find Christmas fancies as you could before the war, but there are some you can make for yourself. Gingerbread men and paper-wrapped toffees will help to fill the children's stockings, and the Christmas cake will look twice as festive with a coating of icing.

GINGERBREAD MEN

Ingredients: 2 oz. sugar or syrup, 2 oz. margarine, 8 oz. plain flour, ½ level teaspoon mixed spice, 2 level teaspoons ginger, lemon substitute, 1 level teaspoon bicarbonate soda. *Method:* Melt in a pan the syrup or sugar and margarine. Pour into a bowl. Add some flour and the spice and lemon substitute. Stir well. Dissolve the bicarbonate of soda in a tablespoon of tepid water and add to the mixture. Continue stirring gradually adding more flour. Finish the process by turning out the mixture on to a well-floured board. Knead in the remainder of the flour. Roll a small ball for the head, flatten it and place it on the baking tin. Roll an oblong for the body and strips for arms and legs. Join these together with a little reconstituted egg and put currants for the eyes.

HONEYCOMB TOFFEE

Ingredients: 2 oz. sugar (demerara if possible), 4 oz. syrup, 2 level teaspoons bicarbonate of soda. *Method:* Boil syrup and sugar together for about 5 minutes, or until it is a rich brown colour. While still boiling stir the bicarbonate of soda in very quickly. Pour into a well-greased sandwich tin, and allow to cool and set. When almost firm, loosen edges with knife and turn out on to wire tray.

ICING *made with ordinary Sugar and Household Milk*

Ingredients: 4 level dessertspoons sugar, 6 level tablespoons Household Milk, dry, 2 tablespoons water, colouring and flavouring. *Method:* Mix sugar and milk together. Add water and beat till smooth. Add colouring and flavouring and spread on top of cake.

THIS IS WEEK 22 — THE SECOND WEEK OF RATION PERIOD No. 6 (Dec. 10th to Jan. 6th)

THE MINISTRY OF FOOD, LONDON, W.1. FOOD FACTS No. 233

Boy Scouts prior to the presentation of a YMCA mobile canteen, Council House, Halesowen, 1942.

Hockey coaching, Pelsall Secondary Modern School, 1951.

Ambassadors of Fine Quality

PARKES
(Regd)

CLASSIC CONFECTIONERY

St. Mary's Girl Guides, St Mary's Road, Bearwood, 1953.

Folk Dancing, Dudley Teachers' Association Festival, 20th July 1951.

Maypole dancing (with a pause for the camera) Mill Street Infants and Junior School, Brierley Hill, 1954.

Playtime at Yew Tree Hill School, Highbridge Road, Netherton, March 1953.

"The Mikado", Halesowen Grammar School December 1954.

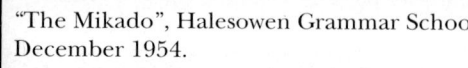

Christmas Party, Adastral Club, Stone Street, Dudley, 1957.

Wolverhampton Municipal Grammar School Girls' Hockey Team, 1958/9.

Snowballing in Dudley Priory ruins, 1st February 1963.

Halesowen Swimming Pool, August 1963.

Library Circle Meeting in the Junior Library, Woodside Branch Library, February 1963.

School camp for Sandwell Boys' School, at
Riversford, c. 1965.

Stephen Martin, aged 8, carefully lines up
shot at the Wolverhampton Company of
Archers' field, The Wergs, Tettenhall, 196

Brierley Hill schoolboys' football team, 1964/5.

Wolverhampton Grammar School Under-13 Cricket Team, Summer 1974.

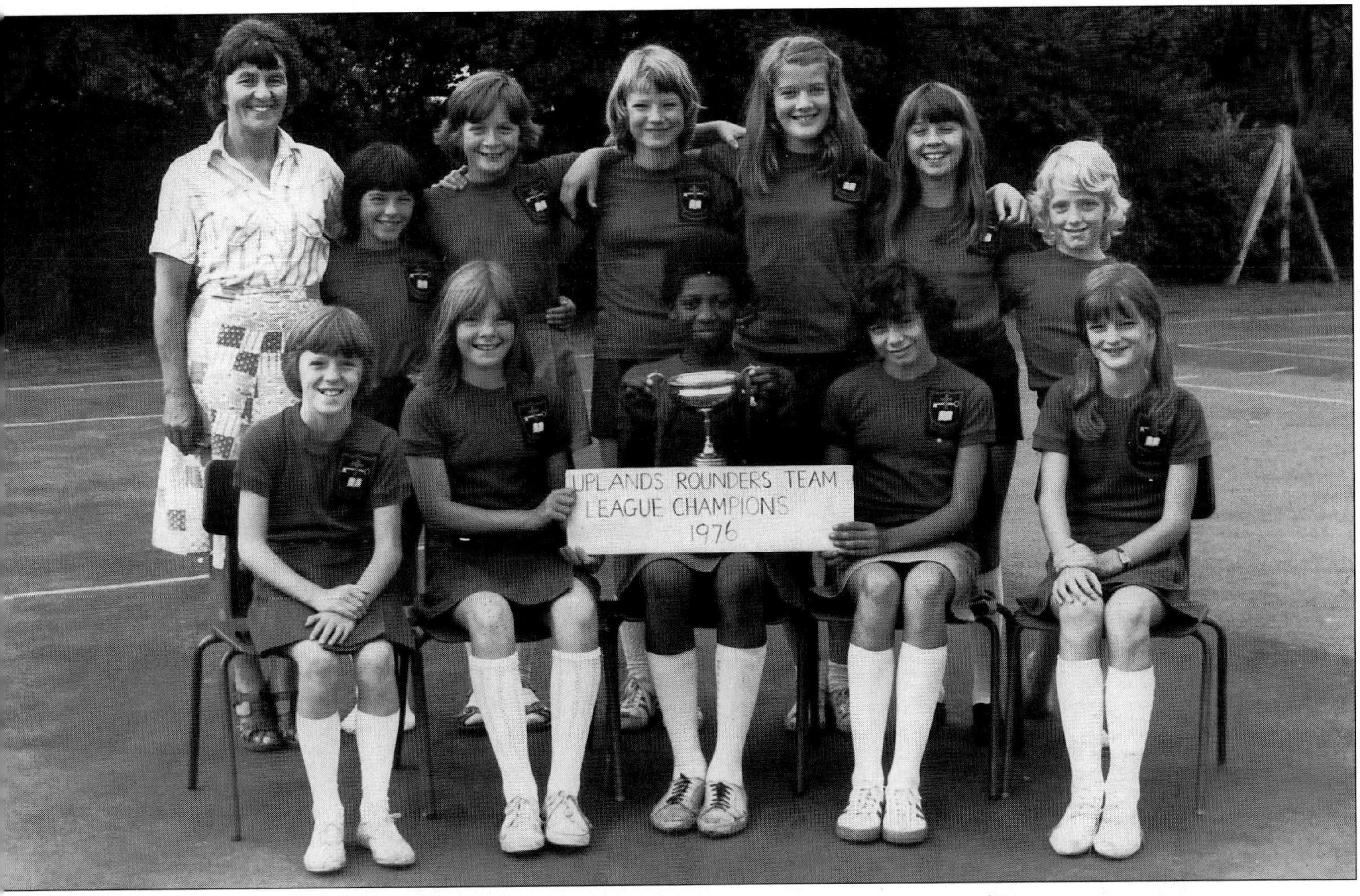
UPLANDS ROUNDERS TEAM
LEAGUE CHAMPIONS
1976

Uplands Junior School, Finchfield, Rounders League Champions, 1976.

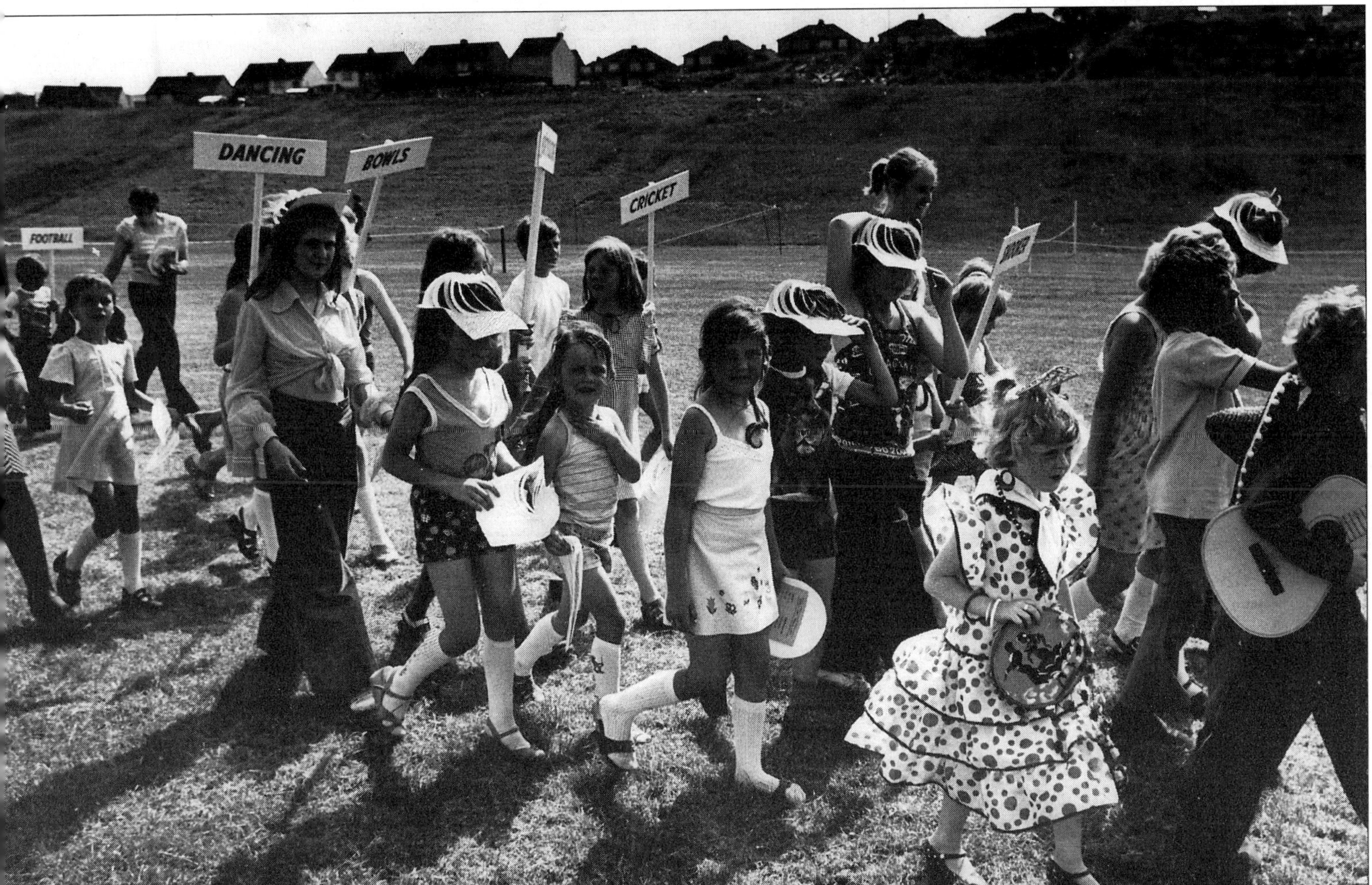
DANCING
BOWLS
CRICKET
FOOTBALL

Fete-goers at the opening of the leisure complex off Brades Rise, Oldbury, 28th June 1976.

Summer activities, organised by Dudley Leisure and Recreation Dept., 1976.

THE BOY'S BRIGADE
BATTALION WELCOME YOU TO

The Boys' Brigade
West Midland
District 10th
Annual Band
Competition
Saturday, May 2nd 1981
at
THE COSELEY SCHOOL
Ivyhouse Lane,
Coseley

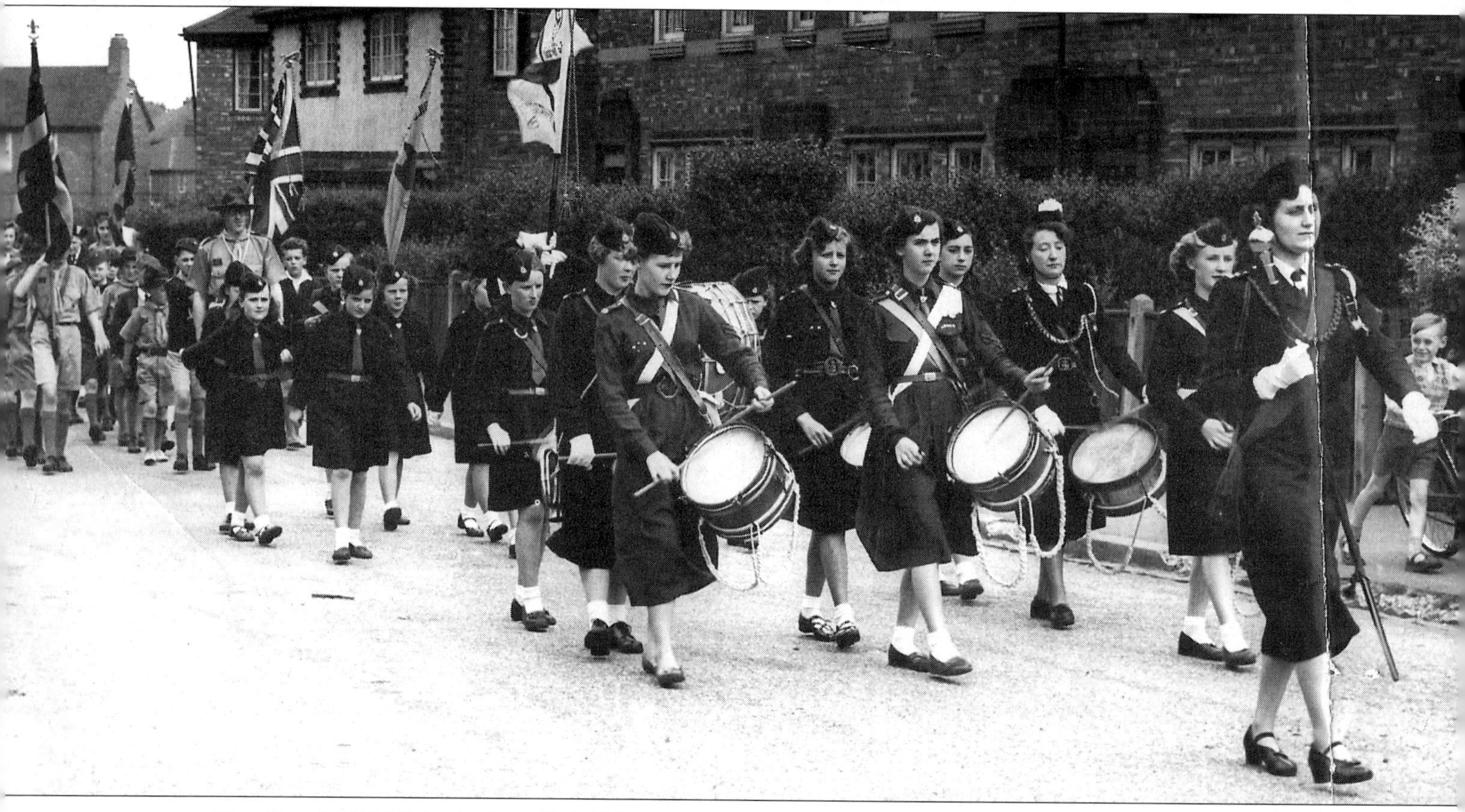

Pupils of Colton Hills Comprehensive School, Wolverhampton, practise
Camp Craft at The Mount, Penn Road, 1980.

The Church Girls' Brigade, from Holy Trinity Church, Ettingshall, take part in a combined church parade, c. 1977.

Some of the youngsters taking part in the Sandwell Junior Passport to Angling competition, staged at the Dartmouth Park and Sandwell Valley Pools, 23rd June 1982.

Albion Starlets' Jazz Band members prepare to lead the Hateley Heath Carnival parade, 7th May 1979.

Young actors from Fir Tree Infants' School, Yew Tree Estate, West Bromwich, meet the Mayor and Mayoress of Sandwell, Coun. and Mrs Jack Smith, after their nativity play performance, 13th December 1984.

Pupils from Rowley Hall, Upland and Parkside Junior Schools, leave Rolfe Street Station, Smethwick, on a special 45 mile round trip, 7th November 1977.

A sponsored "Bounce" on a giant air cushion, Newton Junior and Infants' School, West Bromwich, 28th March 1986.

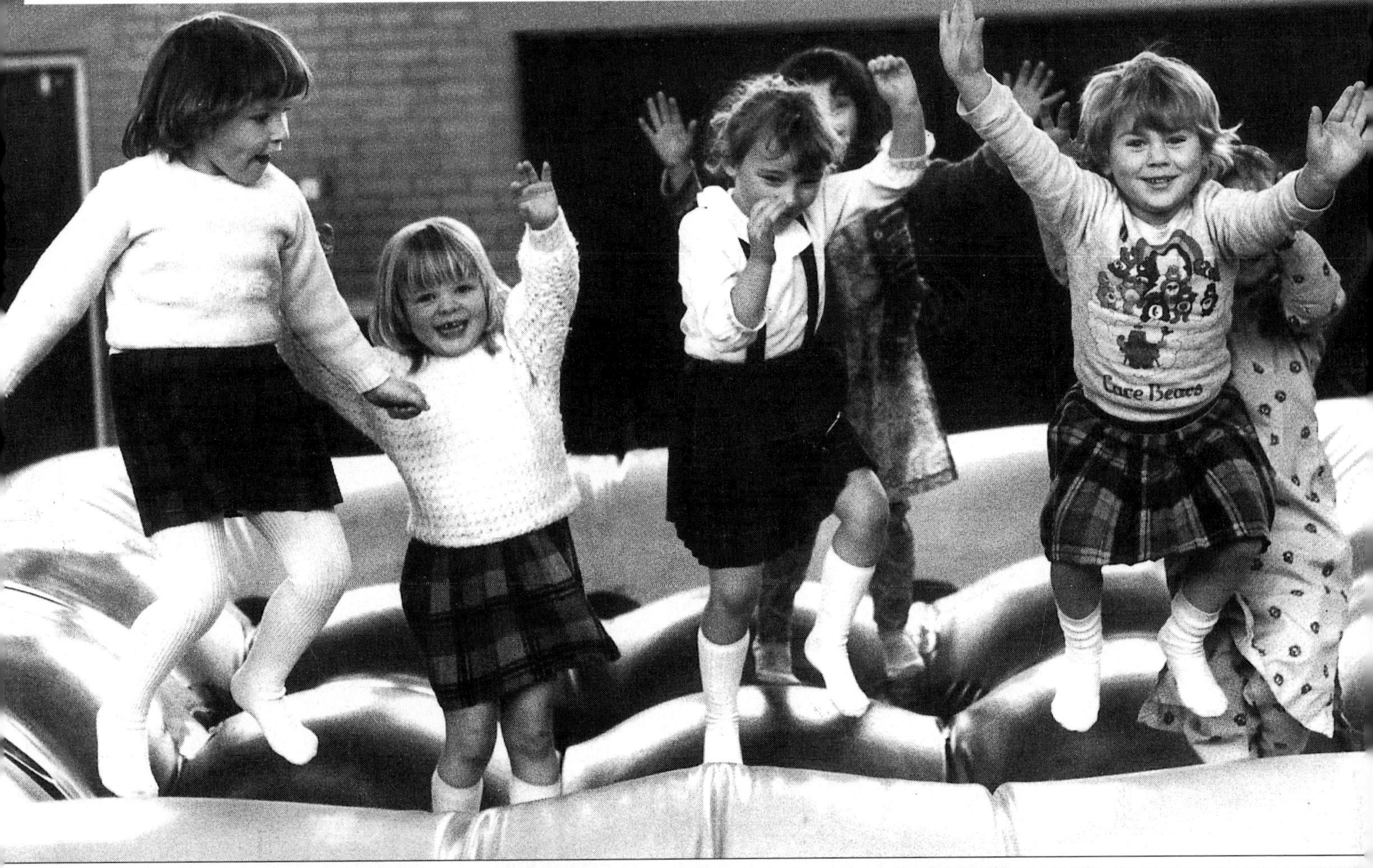

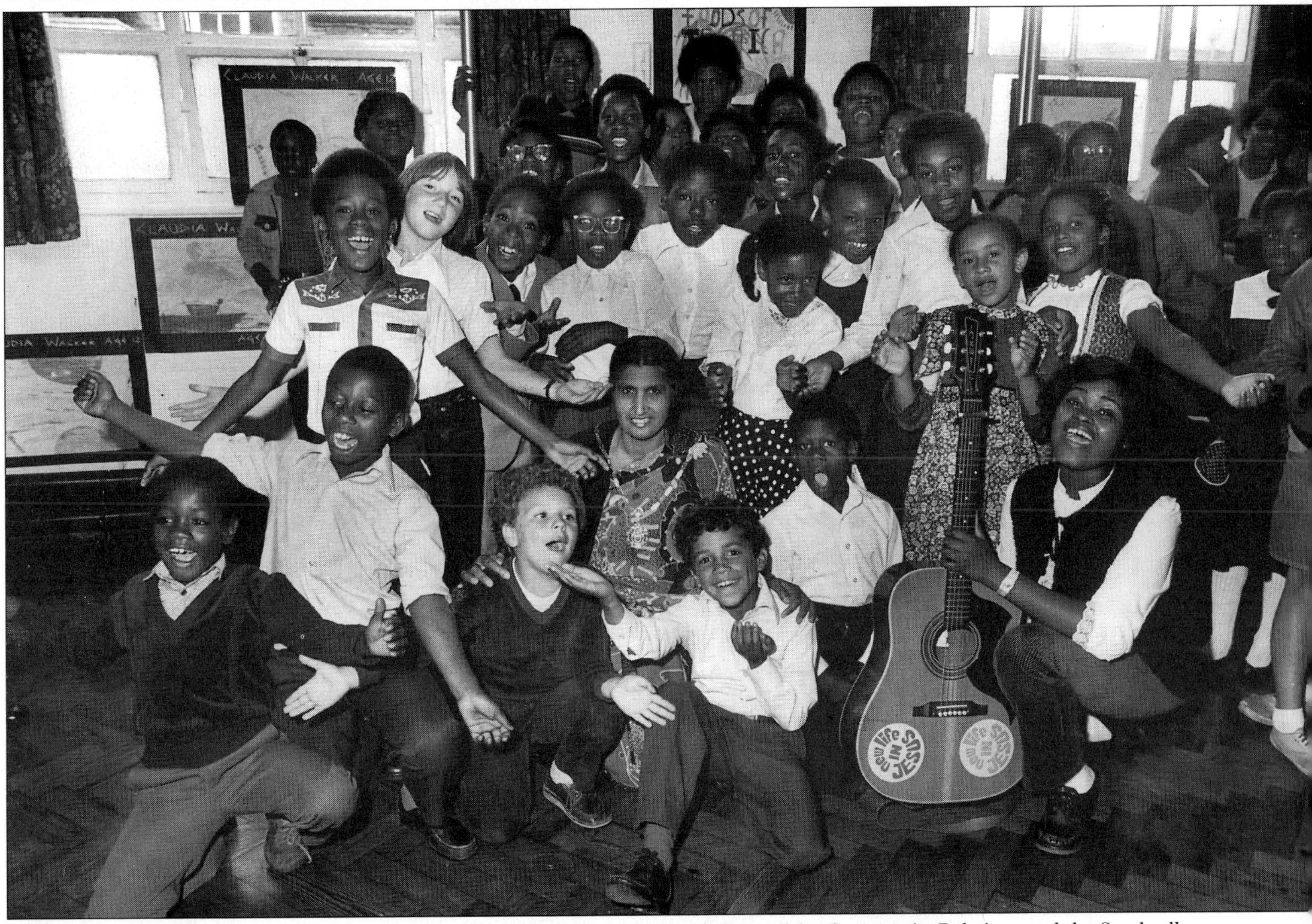

The end of a three week course of art and craft, organised by the Sandwell Council for Community Relations and the Sandwell District West Indian Community Association, brings a fond farewell from some of the children taking part, Lodge Road School, West Bromwich, 20th August 1982.

Enjoyment at the Sandwell Show, King George's Fields, West Bromwich, 26th August 1990.

Brownies take part in their task of making as many cups of tea as possible, in one week, Sun Garage, Sandwell Road, West Bromwich, 1985. It was in aid of the "Save-the-Children" fund.

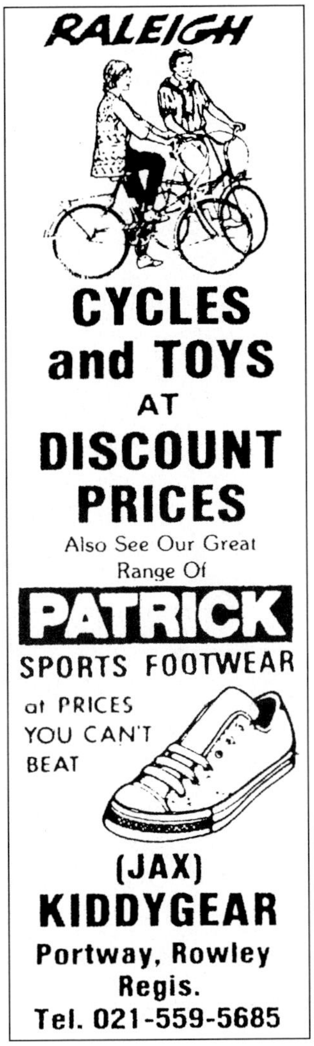

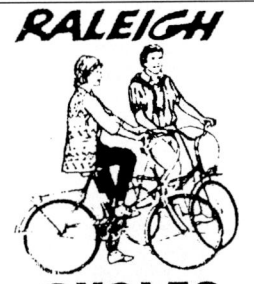

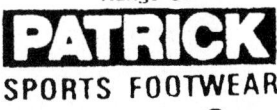

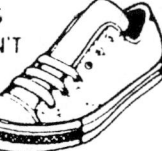

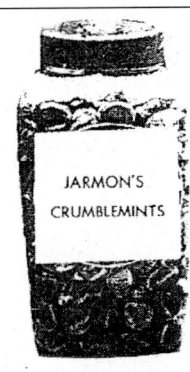

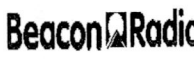

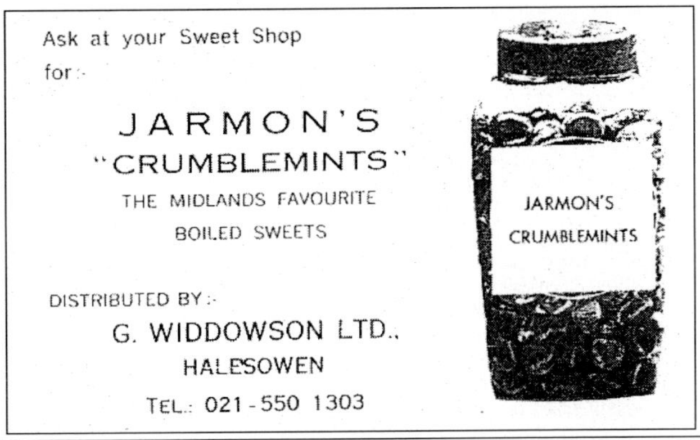

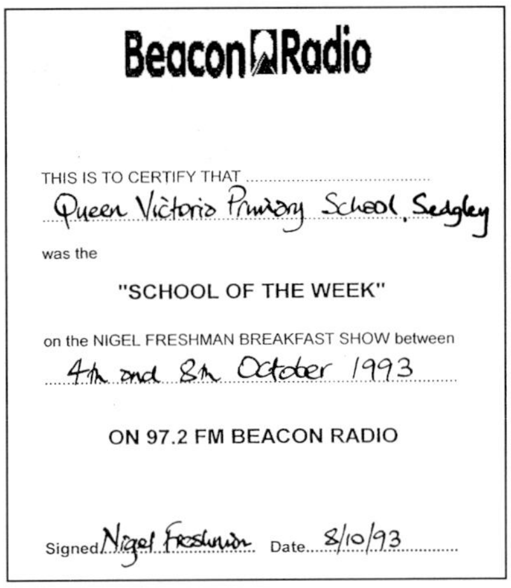
Beacon Radio

THIS IS TO CERTIFY THAT Queen Victoria Primary School, Sedgley

was the

"SCHOOL OF THE WEEK"

on the NIGEL FRESHMAN BREAKFAST SHOW between

4th and 8th October 1993

ON 97.2 FM BEACON RADIO

Signed Nigel Freshman Date 8/10/93

CHILDREN AT RISK PROJECTS

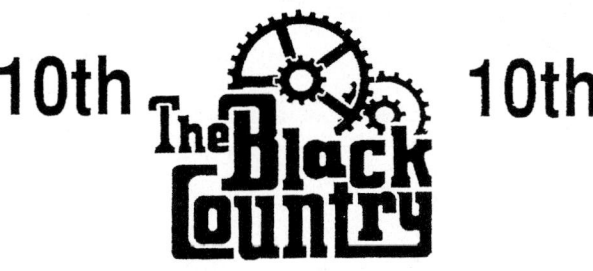

10th The Black Country 10th

Held under AAA Laws & BARR Grade I

HALF MARATHON

SUNDAY 26th June 1994

COMMEMORATIVE AWARDS TO ALL FINISHER'S

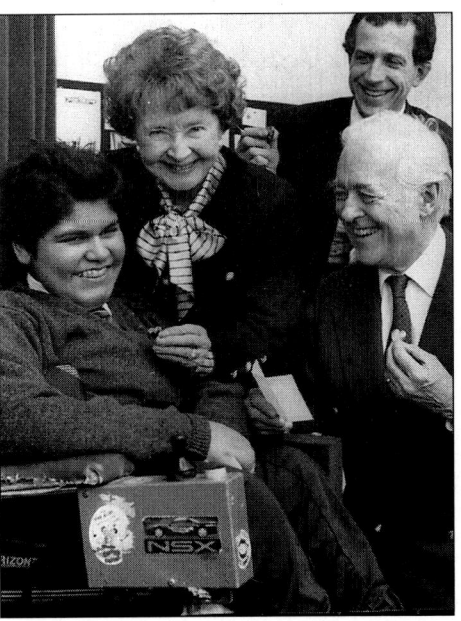

Schoolboy, Harbinder Mann, persuades Michael Denison and Dulcie Gray to wear their hearts on their sleeves for a St. Valentine's Day fund-raiser for the Variety Club campaign, 14th February 1992. The two actors were appearing at the Grand Theatre in "Bedroom Farce." Michael Crump, Head Teacher of Colton Hills School, looks on with approval.

Children from St. Mary Magdalene Church of England Primary School celebrate their triumph in the "Junior Jog" around Churchfields Playing Fields, off Church Vale, West Bromwich, 7th May 1986.

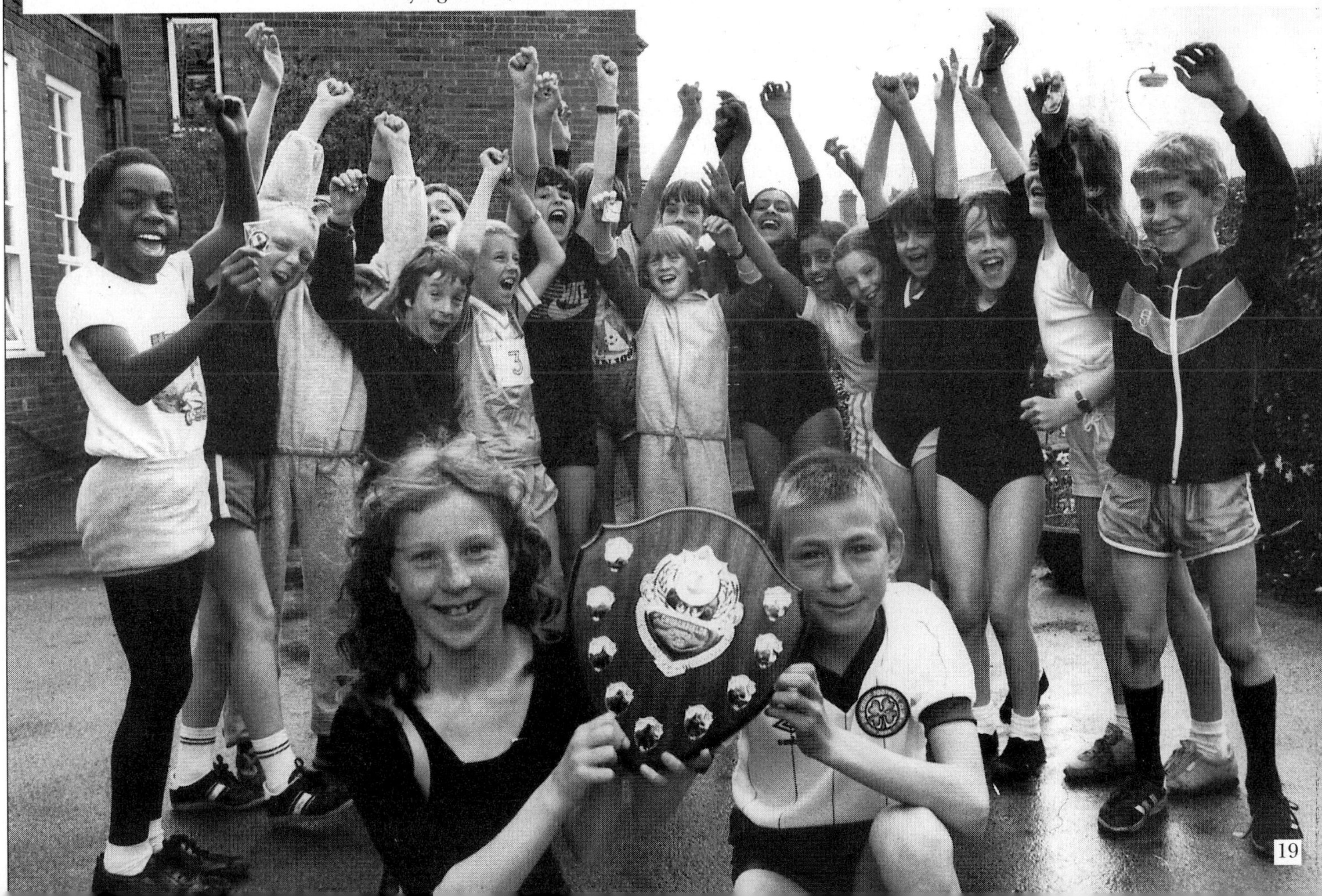

SOMETHING SPECIAL

Wally Davies, a Dudley inventor, with his own aircraft, Priory Fields, Dudley, 4th August 1911.

CORONATION
OF
KING GEORGE V. & QUEEN MARY
JUNE 22nd, 1911.

Programme OF Festivities

For Kingswinford and Wall Heath,
In the Grounds adjoining Summerhill
Court,
Kindly lent by Mr. H. Sidney Pitt.

PROGRAMMES, ONE PENNY EACH.

—OFFICERS :—

Chairman of Committee ... ... Rev. R. H. Streeten
Vice-Chairman ... ... Councillor G. Meanley
Treasurer ... ... Mr. James Horne
Chairman of Sports' Committee ... Councillor J. B. Webb
Vice-Chairman " " ... ... Mr. C. H. Clewley
Secretaries ... { Noah Mathews, Market Street
{ Harry Phillips, St. Mary's School

GOD SAVE THE KING.

W. H. FELLOWS, PRINTER, KINGSWINFORD.

Coronation Day, Green Lane, Walsall, 22nd June 1911.

The employees of D. Mason & Sons about to embark on their annual outing, this time from Walsall to Evesham, c. 1924. It is interesting to see that the speed limit of the vehicle was 12 m.p.h.

Brierley Hill Carnival in the late 1920's.

Halesowen residents set off on a coach tour, 1927.

The Mayor inspects the Guard of Honour of ex-servicemen, Walsall Hospital's Carnival, 1930.

All ready for the May Day Parade, Queen Street, Walsall, c. 1935.

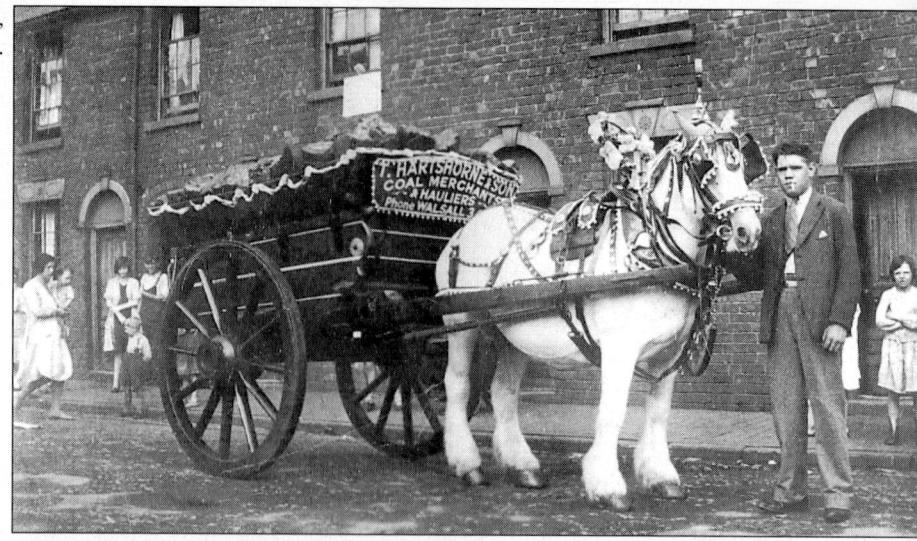

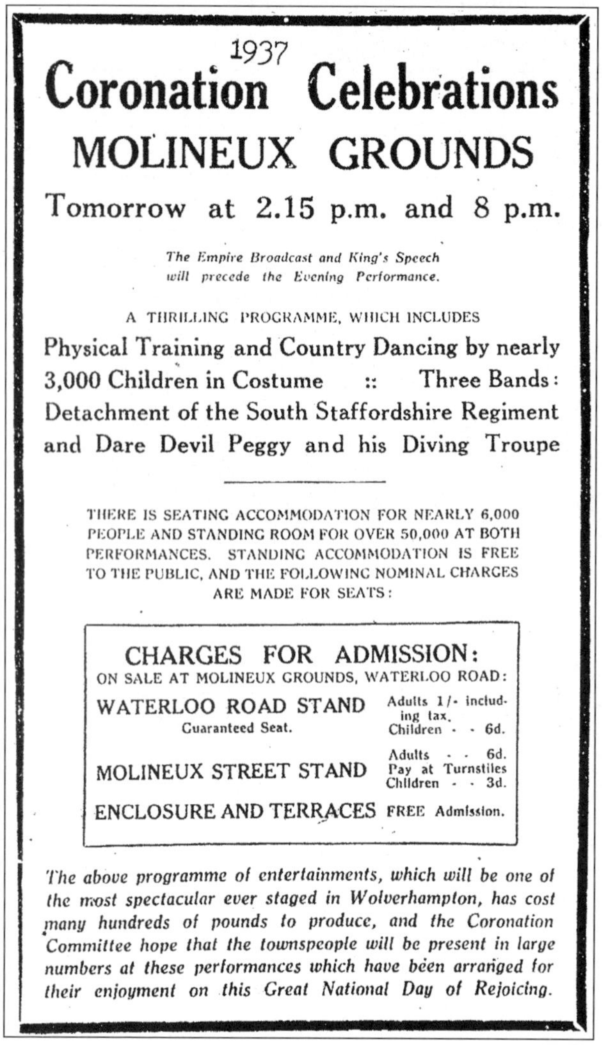

1937

Coronation Celebrations

MOLINEUX GROUNDS

Tomorrow at 2.15 p.m. and 8 p.m.

The Empire Broadcast and King's Speech will precede the Evening Performance.

A THRILLING PROGRAMME, WHICH INCLUDES

Physical Training and Country Dancing by nearly 3,000 Children in Costume :: Three Bands: Detachment of the South Staffordshire Regiment and Dare Devil Peggy and his Diving Troupe

THERE IS SEATING ACCOMMODATION FOR NEARLY 6,000 PEOPLE AND STANDING ROOM FOR OVER 50,000 AT BOTH PERFORMANCES. STANDING ACCOMMODATION IS FREE TO THE PUBLIC, AND THE FOLLOWING NOMINAL CHARGES ARE MADE FOR SEATS:

CHARGES FOR ADMISSION:
ON SALE AT MOLINEUX GROUNDS, WATERLOO ROAD:

WATERLOO ROAD STAND Guaranteed Seat.	Adults 1/- including tax. Children - - 6d.
MOLINEUX STREET STAND	Adults - - 6d. Pay at Turnstiles Children - - 3d.
ENCLOSURE AND TERRACES	FREE Admission.

The above programme of entertainments, which will be one of the most spectacular ever staged in Wolverhampton, has cost many hundreds of pounds to produce, and the Coronation Committee hope that the townspeople will be present in large numbers at these performances which have been arranged for their enjoyment on this Great National Day of Rejoicing.

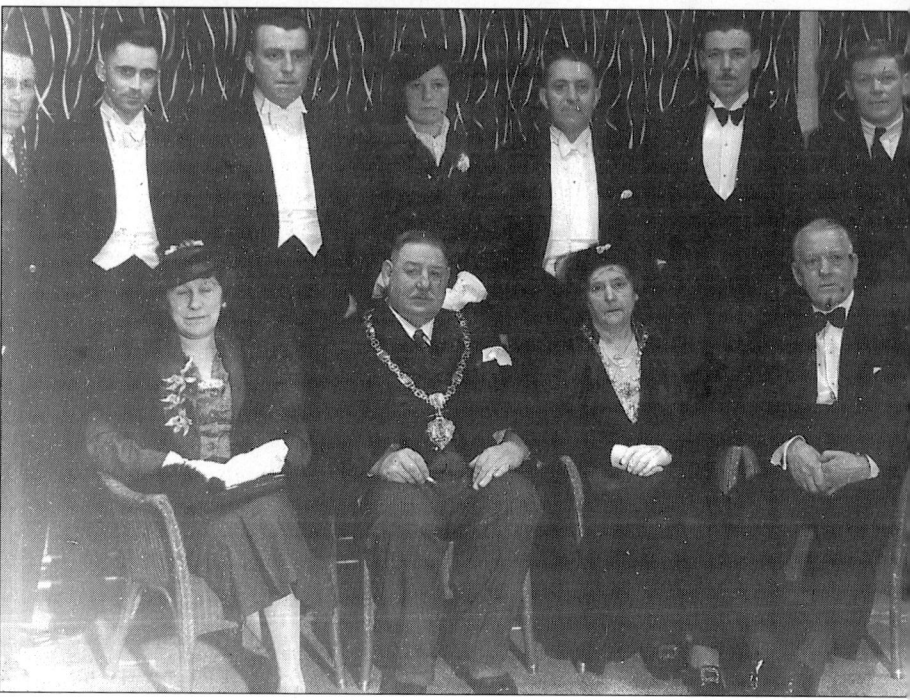

The civic party, including the Mayor and Mayoress of Halesowen, Alderman and Mrs Downing, at the opening of the Lyttleton Cinema, 16th April 1938.

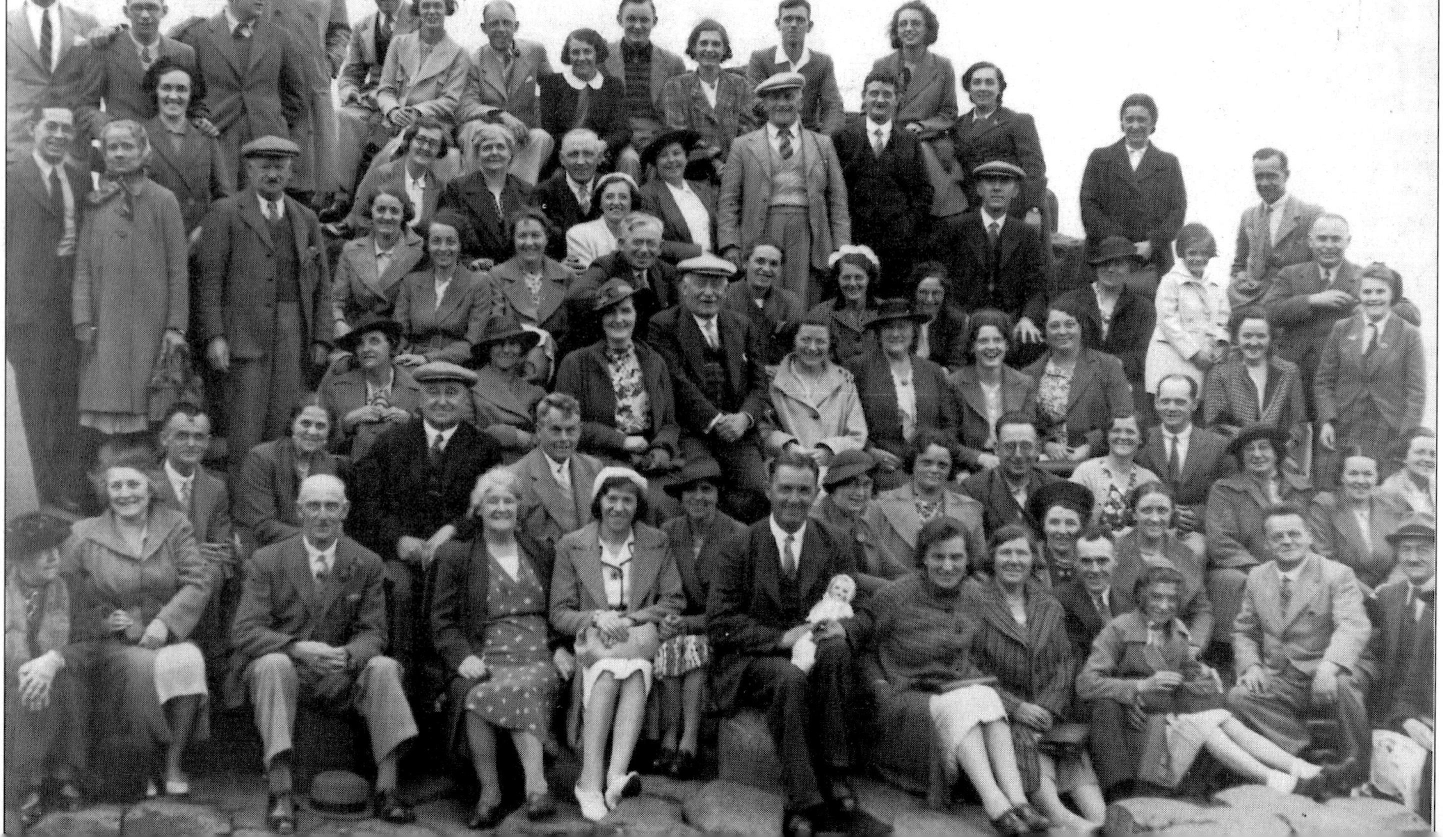

Holidaymakers from Walsall and the surrounding areas, at Giant's Causeway, Northern Ireland, August 1939.

Opening ceremony at the Woodside Sons of Rest, c. 1946.

Shopping week, High Street, Brierley Hill, 1951. This was part of the Festival of Britain celebrations.

St. Mary's Church bazaar, Bearwood, 1951.

The Chairman of the Brierley Hill
Urban District Council
(Councillor H. C. Roberts, J.P., B.Sc., A.C.I.S.)
and
The Chairman of the Sedgley
Urban District Council
(Councillor Mrs. E. E. Williams, J.P., C.C.)

request the pleasure of the company of

Mr. H. WOODWARD & LADY

at a Civic Reception to the Brierley Hill
and Sedgley Schools' Football Team and
the Brierley Hill Alliance Football Team
at the Town Hall, Brierley Hill on
Friday, 15th June, 1951 at 7 p.m.

Dress Informal.

R.S.V.P. by 12th June, to :-
The Clerk of the Council,
Moor Street,
Brierley Hill.

Quarry Bank Festival Gala Committee, Quarry Bank Park, 14th July 1951.

Coronation procession, Stourbridge Road, Woodside, Dudley, 1953.

Coronation Parade of Police and Quarry Bank Silver Band to Marsh Park, Brierley Hill, 31st May 1953.

NALGO Dinner Dance, Gala Baths, West Bromwich, c. 1952.

31,000 See TV at West Bromwich

3.6.53

Quiet Day Until Teatime Parties Started

It is estimated that about 30,000 West Bromwich people saw the Coronation ceremony on television in their own homes or sharing facilities with relatives or friends. In addition nearly 1,000, mostly old people and widows, saw the ceremony on 11 sets provided at the Town Hall.

There was little outdoor activity until towards tea-time when hundreds of children in all parts of the town assembled for the parties for which funds had been collected and preparations made during many weeks. Tables were laid in party yards, public-house yards and even on street pavements.

Where fields or other suitable open spaces were not available streets were used for organised games. Some parties had their own bonfires and firework displays, and revelry in which adults eventually joined.

A Midland Red departure, from Bearwood, leads to a sunny scene at Land's End, 18th August 1953. This was just one of the company's South Crest and West Country tours.

BEWILDERED

An enthusiast of church history and churches was " doing " one in a Black Country town, and was being followed round by a somewhat old and seedy man who from time to time called attention to interesting features.

The stranger was grateful, and enquired tactfully of the man what connection he had with the church.

" Well, it's like this," he replied. " The old parson who was 'ere years and years ago used to call me 'sextant'; then another one come, and he called me the 'beetle,' and now the present one says I'm the 'virgin,' and between 'em I'm d—— if I know what I am."

Aquarium Gift to Walsall Hospital

5/8/53

An aquarium of tropical fish was presented to Walsall General Hospital on Tuesday by members of Walsall Aquatic Society. It will be placed in Hale Ward where the patients are young children. The gift was handed over by Mrs. S. Millis-Clark, president of the society.

Halesowen scouts, Kenneth Arnold and Colin Coley, meet the Deputy Mayor, Coun. Southall, prior to setting off for a Jamboree in Canada, 20th June 1955.

Opening of part of the canal for pleasure boating, "The Leasowes", Halesowen, 23rd July 1955, by the Mayor and Mayoress Coun. and Mrs Spring.

Christmas Party, Clydesdale Stamping Co., Netherton, 10th January 1958.

Smethwick Ladies' Harriers collecting for Smethwick Carnival, 22nd May 1954.

Mr Payne, the Founder Member, cuts the first sod for the building of Shenstone Club, Kent Road, Halesowen, 4th September 1954.

Students' Carnival Rag Day, Dudley, 12th May 1956.

Bank Staff and their guests at the Civic Hall, Wolverhampton, in 1958, celebrate the Silver Jubilee of the Wolverhampton & District Trustee Savings Bank.

Opening ceremony at Wordsley Youth Club,
14th May 1960.

The site being cleared for Wordsley Scouts' new hut,
October 1958.

481 (West Bromwich) Squadron, Air Training Corps, enjoy their
annual summer camp at RAF Wittering, 15th August 1960.

"THE BROOK" LAGOON

Wordsley Gala, 13th July 1963.

Members of the South Staffs branches of the Workers Education Association after a trip through the Dudley tunnel, 1963.

Members of Dudley Amateur Radio Club set up a portable station, May 1964.

Crowning of the Gala Queen, Quarry Bank Carnival, 1963.

Wall Heath Queen's Scouts, 28th March 1964.

The Mayor, Coun. Caleb Homer, uses a Bean Car at the opening of the Black Country Exhibition, Dudley, August 1967.

The opening of the ground floor Fiction section, Dudley Central Library, 10th March 1966.

Ted Gibson of Finchfield, Wolverhampton, takes a pupil for a flying lesson, Halfpenny Green Airport, Nr. Stourbridge, 1966.

Moving the stock to the new library, Halesowen, 1971.

WEST BROMWICH RESIDENTIAL ARTS CENTRE
INGESTRE HALL

PARTNERSCHULE DES WILLIGIS-GYMNASIUMS
ZU MAINZ

KONZERT

DES WEST BROMWICH YOUTH ORCHESTRA

MITTWOCH, 30. AUGUST 1967, 20 UHR

KURFÜRSTLICHES SCHLOSS ZU MAINZ
GROSSER SAAL

**West Bromwich Youth Orchestra,
19th September 1967.**

Give him the real thing a steam engine by Mamod.

Magnificent Mamod working steam models are built to give lasting pleasure. A wide range of fabulous road vehicles, stationary engines and accessories to suit boys of all ages, at prices to suit every pocket. Available at leading toy and model shops now!

Ever fascinating steam from

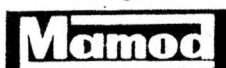

Malins (Mamod) Ltd., Brierley Hill, West Midlands.

Alice Cooper puts the finishing touches to a model of a steam engine, Malins (Mamod) Ltd., Brierley Hill, 1969.

'First wet day in 23 years' 20/8/70

Scores of handicapped people from Warley set off on their "big day out" today in pouring rain but with high spirits — and a special escort.

Officials of the Smethwick Cripples' Welfare and Outing Fund made special arrangements with the Automobile Association for a fully equipped vehicle to follow the fleet of 11 coaches to and from Wickstead Park, near Kettering.

Mrs. Olive Holloway, secretary of the fund, said: "This is the 23rd annual outing and this is the first day it has been wet."

£1,000 from pubs goes to old people 1971

A cheque for £1,000 raised by a tote run by the "Pubs Effort Committee" was formally handed over to Bloxwich Carnival Committee.

The money is to be used, together with other cash raised by the Carnival Committee, for cash gifts and a mammoth party and a night's entertainment for the old people of Bloxwich.

240 (Darlaston) Squadron, Air Training Corps, attend summer camp at RAF West Raynham, Summer 1973.

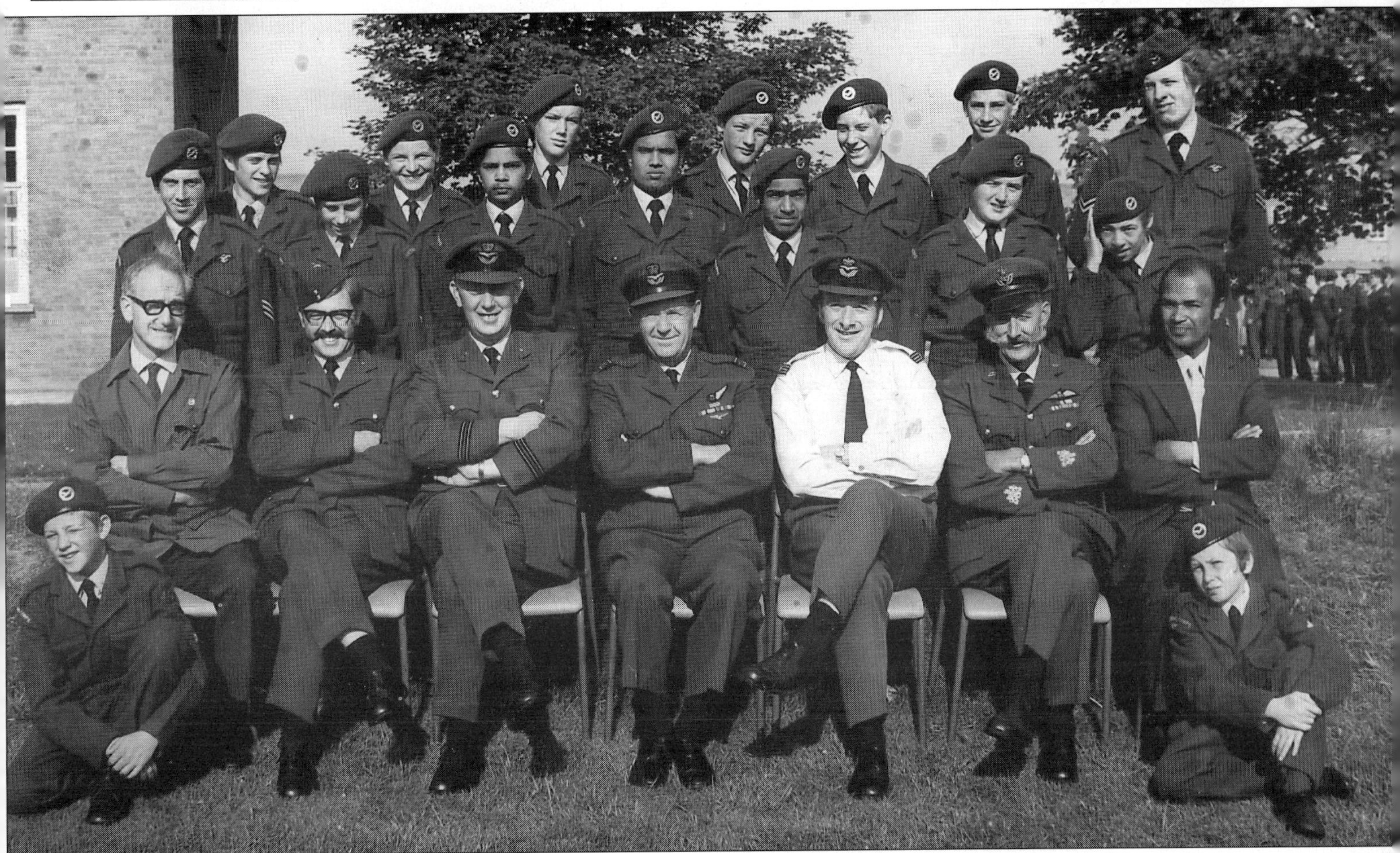

Penn Choral Society, Wolverhampton, take part in the Llangollen International Musical Eisteddfod, 11th July 1975.

On her Silver Jubilee visit to Dudley, the Queen is greeted by the crowd in happy mood, outside the Conservative Club in Priory Road, 1977.

Inkberrow Road residents celebrate the Queen's Silver Jubilee, Halesowen, 6th June 1977.

35

Silver Jubilee celebrations, Barston Road, Oldbury, 1977.

Tom Bennett, Rachael Heyhoe-Flint and Dennis Moore, the winning team from BBC TV's regional quiz programme, "Know Your Place", present the Mayor of Woverhampton, Coun. H.E. 'Ted' Lane with the trophy, 24th April 1981.

The Arboretum entrance, Walsall, 1979.

The first Sandwell Historic Vehicle Show, Sandwell Valley, 14th May 1978.

Contestants in the Miss Europe competition "leg it" through Dudley Tunnel, 1981.

Winnie Price hands over a cheque to The Guide Dogs for the Blind Association, c. 1982. Workers at Sankeys took part in sponsored walks, on ten occasions, from Kinver Edge to Lanesfield, raising enough money to buy a dog each time.

Ada McCall cuts the cake to celebrate the launch of a community-authored book, "Something to Warm Us Up", Littlemore Hill, 7th March 1984. The book was penned by 35 pensioners from Hillcrest, Church Vale, Beechcroft and Kings Meadow old people's homes.

Ivy Hancock, who has organised charity shows for 50 years, with member of her "Evergreens" concert party, 14th June 1983. She had just been in ed to Buckingham Palace in recognition of her work. Originally she fou ed the group at Great Bridge Street Methodist Church, Swan Village.

Helpers at the Clarkes Lane Old People's Home, West Bromwich, take part in a fair (which raised £220 to buy a stereo unit) 1st December 1984.

Air Training Corps

Certificate of Training

This is to Certify that

Cadet   M MOORE
of No.   481 (WEST BROMWICH)   Squadron
has qualified as a Leading Cadet by
obtaining a   CREDIT
in the Leading Cadet Examination.

Commandant
Air Training Corps

Dated this   6   day of   NOVEMBER   19 89

FRIDAY 26 JUNE
10.00am-4.00pm
WALSALL TOWN HALL

A FREE DAY OF FITNESS, FUN AND FACT, ESPECIALLY FOR THE OLDER PERSON

★ ANTIQUES ROAD SHOW - Bring your antiques for valuation ★ PET CARE ADVICE ★ GARDENING ADVICE ★ HEALTH AND FITNESS ★ ARTS AND CRAFTS ★ HAIR AND BEAUTY ★ Entertainment from WALSALL HOSPITAL RADIO ★ SENIOR CITIZENS ORCHESTRA Plus special appearance by **ALTON DOUGLAS**

WH SMITH

An inflatable spider takes to the water, together with a live Dudley Zoo tarantula, Tipton Swimming and Leisure Centre, 1989.

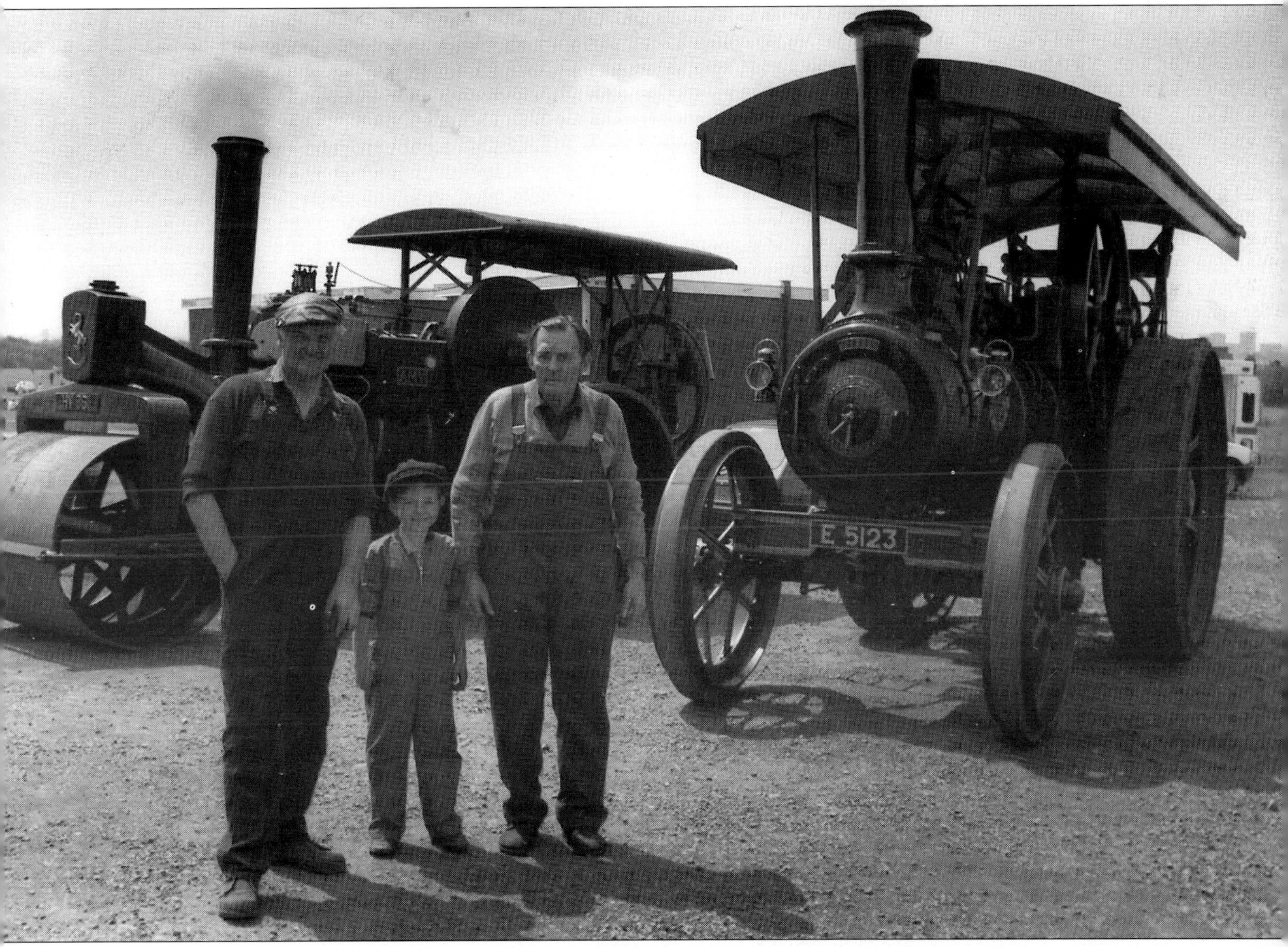

Walsall County Fair, The Airport, Aldridge Road, 1993.

Tea Dance, Walsall Town Hall, 1994.

Tom Holmes with part of his collection of Kipper ties, the
largest in the world, The People's Show, Walsall, 1993.

Midland Bus
& Commercial Show

WALSALL   ARBORETUM,   WALSALL,   WEST MIDLANDS

SUNDAY, 26TH JUNE, 1994

PLAY UP! PLAY UP! AND PLAY THE GAME!

FOOTBALL.

THE FIRST
GENERAL MEETING
OF THE
GOLDTHORN
FOOTBALL CLUB

Will (by the kind permission of the Vicar) be held at

ST. LUKE'S SCHOOL,
BLAKENHALL,

Friday next, November 10, 1876,

AT 7.30 P.M.

Any Gentleman interested in the game is invited to attend.

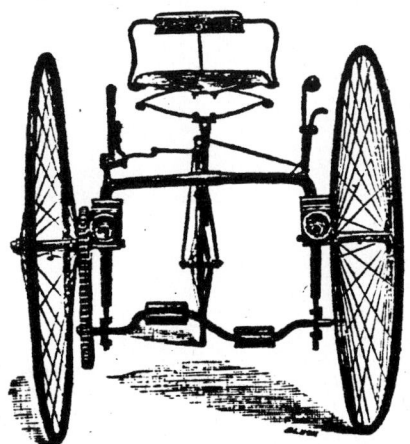

Wolverhampton Early Closing Association Football Team, 1895/96.

Members of Miss Anstey's Physical Training College, The Leasowes, Halesowen, 1904.

Dudley Conservative Bowling Club, c. 1905.

Wolverhampton Excelsior Cycling Club, West Park, 1910.

Wolverhampton Excelsior FC, 1911/12.

Walsall Football News

The Official Programme of the Walsall Football Club.

No. 12.   SATURDAY, DECEMBER 4, 1920.   PRICE 2D.

PARTIES desirous of booking a char-a-banc or private car for Walsall's away matches, should apply for terms to

THE SPRINGHILL GARAGE,
AUTOMOBILE AND MOTOR ENGINEERS.
EALING HOUSE,
Upper Bridge St., - - WALSALL.

Telegrams : "Scooter" Walsall. . . Telephones : 164 & 658.

Printed by the "Pioneer" Press, Lichfield Street, Walsall.

Menzies High School Cricket Eleven, West Bromwich, c. 1913.

Members of Bloxwich/Walsall Cyclists' Touring Club, c. 1929.

Opening of the new baths, Blowers Green, Dudley, 1926.

WOLVERHAMPTON workers played a major part in the attempt on the world land speed record of 1930.

The world attempt was made by The Silver Bullet, built by hand by local men employed at The Sunbeam Motor Car Company. The Wolverhampton mechanics went to America for the project.

The world record was determined by an average speed of two each way runs, which took place on Daytona Beach, Florida, in March, 1930. The Bullet achieved this on its first run, but unfortunately the exhaust blew on its return, depriving the local men of £100 bonus each.

The event was covered by all the newspapers, newsreels, both in this country and in America.

Wolverhampton Wanderers FC Playing Staff, 1925/26.

West Bromwich Albion players and staff, at the railway station, prior to setting off for Wembley and F.A. Cup glory, 1931.

ALBION'S SPARKLING SEASON. 2.5.31

CUP AND PROMOTION!

NO MORE "SECOND" FARE AT HAWTHORNS.

ONE of the greatest football "doubles" has materialised! Albion, the pride of the Black Country—and the Midlands—have won the Cup and Promotion. Albion's feat deserves—and will—rank with the performances of Preston North End (in 1888-9) and Aston Villa (in 1896-7) in winning the Cup and the League championship in the same season.

There were jubilant scenes at The Hawthorns to-day. Prior to the beginning of the match a new Flag of Victory was unfurled in front of the stand in the presence of the Cup victors and 50,000 of their admirers. That ceremony over Albion proceeded to qualify for return to the First Division by beating Charlton Athletic.

Charlton were irksome rivals of Albion as they were in the Cup in the early days of January. They took the lead, lost it and regained it but the Cup holders lasted the better. Albion's vital victory was hard-earned and almost as popular as their triumph at Wembley last week.

Bringing Home the Cup

UNPRECEDENTED SCENES AT WELCOME TO TEAM 2.5.31

Scenes without precedent in the history of West Bromwich were witnessed when the Cup was brought home on Monday. Thousands of enthusiastic admirers gave the team a rousing send-off from Paddington, and at Snow Hill Station another huge crowd welcomed them. On behalf of the Birmingham County F.A. a handsome bouquet was presented to Mrs. Bassett, the wife of the Chairman of Directors, and the engine which drew the train was gaily decorated. At every subsequent station and at vantage points along the line crowds assembled and cheered wildly. A huge concourse had assembled on the platforms at West Bromwich and as the players stepped out of the train they were received by the Mayor and members of the Town Council. The appearance of Glidden carrying the Cup was the signal for an outburst of cheering. Char-a-bancs were in waiting and a procession was formed, the central feature being the captain of the team seated on the top of one vehicle with his comrades around him and the Cup prominently displayed. A band headed the triumphant march, and the jazz band from Kenrick & Jefferson's brought up the rear.

Albion Lose Record

Wolves 3, West Bromwich 2

THE Wolves, losing by two goals at the interval, fought back gallantly and ultimately defeated their Black Country rivals, West Bromwich Albion, by the odd goal in five.

Wolves, who made many changes, played improved football, but in the first half the forwards still suffered from their old fault of bad finishing. Clarke and Johnson scored the Albion's goals.

The visitors were unlucky in losing Gripton late in the first half. He got concussion when heading the ball, but was able to resume after the interval on the right wing.

Tranter, who went into the middle of the Albion's defence, made a strong substitute, but the visitors missed Gripton's steadying influence, and late in the game he resumed his old place. While he was on the right wing, Acquroff beat Lewis twice, and Crook won the game for the Wolves in the sixty-fourth minute. And so the Albion lost their unbeaten away record. 19.11.44

PRICE ONE PENNY

THE WOLVES
Official Programme

Saturday, Feb. 28th, 1942.   Kick-off 3-0 p.m.
INTER-ALLIED SERVICES CUP COMPETITION (Round 1)

NAMES AND POSITIONS OF PLAYERS.
BELGIAN ARMY IN GREAT BRITAIN
Colours - Shirts, Red.   Knickers, Black.

RIGHT   M. HUWAERT   LEFT
(1)
A. CRICKELIE   C. LEGRAND
(2)   (3)
A. WILLEMS   R. BILLET   G. VAN DEN BOSSCH
(4)   (5)   (6)
M. KENENS   E. DE BUSSER   A. LANDRIEU   J. SCHUERMANS   A. CLERINCKX
(7)   (8)   (9)   (10)   (11)

Referee—   Linesmen—
W. H. CLINTON   Red Stripe P. Vrydag (Belgian Army)
(Wolverhampton)   Blue Stripe F/Lt. J. B. Birkhead, R.A.F.

.F/LT. F. RILEY   F/SGT. A. H. GIBBONS   SGT. R. S. ANDERSON
(10)   (9)   (8)
(England & Corinthians)   (England & Spurs.)   (England & Dulwich)
F/SGT. L. C. FINCH   SGT. G. COLLINS
(11)   (7)
(England & Barnet.)   (R.A.F.)
A.C. R. E. WRIGHT   P/O B JOY   CPL. T. H. LEEK
(6)   (5)   (4)
(England & Walthamstow)   (England & Arsenal)   (England & Moor Green)
SGT. G. SERGEANT   SGT. W. WHITTAKER
(3)   (2)
(F.A. XI & Romford)   (England & Kingstonian)
LEFT   SGT. B. F. WILLIAMS   RIGHT
(1)
(Walsall)

R.A.F. AMATEUR XI
Colours—Shirts, Blue   Knickers, Dark.
THE TEAMS ARE SUBJECT TO ALTERATION

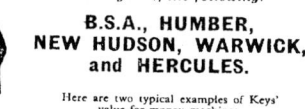

Wolverhampton Grammar School First Eleven Cricket Team (plus twelfth man), 1945.

Dick Turpin.

Llew Forrest, Brierley Hill butcher, demonstrates his skill, driving pony and Hackney gig, Kingswinford Show, 1946.

The meeting of West Bromwich Albion and Aston Villa to-morrow reminds me that 50 years ago this local Derby marked the last playing season for the Albion of "Joe" Reader, one of the last goalkeepers in the country to wear long trousers.

On Monday, "Joe" still hale and hearty, will celebrate the 84th anniversary of his birthday which, incidentally, coincides with the completion of 65 years' service with the club. For more than 30 years he has been steward in charge of the directors' seats at The Hawthorns where his tall, straight figure, much belying his years, can be seen every Saturday.

Reader, who was born at Carters Green, West Bromwich, hade his first appearance for the Albion in 1885 when he was 19, and he holds the record of having played in the club's colours on three of their grounds—Four Acres, Stoney Lane and The Hawthorns.

He kept goal for the Albion in the last Cup Final played at the Oval in 1892 when they beat Villa 3—0, and in the first Cup Final at Crystal Palace in 1895 when the

in his hey-day the best all-rounder who ever played for the club. During the 22 full seasons he played for its first eleven in the Birmingham League he scored just fewer than 8,000 runs, an excellent average of over 350 runs a season. His most successful campaign was 1910, when he aggregated 733 runs in 14 completed innings for an average of 52.35, topping the Birmingham League batting averages and scoring more runs than any player in the league.

Four centuries he made that season included 133 against Mitchells and Butlers, the highest league score of his career. Altogether he scored ten league centuries. Though pre-eminently a batsman, his prowess with the ball was of no mean order, and in all he secured nearly 500 wickets in First Division matches.

He was an accomplished slip-fielder, as was his brother, the late Mr. W. G. Gethin; two other brothers, H. M. and H. S., also assisted the club's first eleven. The Gethin tradition has been strong in Kidderminster cricket, representatives of three succeeding generations having served the club as chairman. *24.2.50*

STRAIGHT FROM THE HORSE'S BACK 1950

COLLECTING old horse brasses is the unusually interesting hobby of Miss Dorothea Isherwood, of 8, Horseley-road, Tipton,

So far, after 11 years' collecting, Miss Isherwood has secured some 180 brasses, including martindales, top-knots, swingers, and name plates.

Her earliest brass is a specimen dating from the beginning of the 19th century.

"All my brasses are genuine, and many of them were bought directly from "the horse's back," claims Miss Isherwood. Often if a new brass is found locally an exchange is arranged between collectors.

Some of Miss Isherwood's best brasses have been "spotted" on cart and canal horses, whose drivers take pride in keeping their animals smart and well-turned-out.

Horse brasses date back many centuries to the time when wagoners used them to decorate the harness of their horses.

Williams turns pro 1952

REX WILLIAMS, 18-year-old Blackheath snooker prodigy turned professional and made his TV debut.

At 17 he had been the youngest player ever to win the English amateur snooker championship.

And it had only been five years since he first picked up a cue.

PRESENTS

SEVENTH ANNUAL
Midland Junior
GRAND PRIX ROAD RACE
(Under British League of Racing Cyclists' Rules)

Sunday, 12th August 1951

START : Market Place, Wolverhampton, 10-30 a.m.

FINISH : Wood Road, Tettenhall, 12-30 approx.

Distance 48 miles

THE COURSE : Wolverhampton - Gailey - St. George's Bye-Pass Shifnal - Bridgnorth - Hermitage Hill (Prime) Compton - Holloway - Tettenhall.

Note.—The Race will be neutralized from the Start, until the "Ball of Coven" on the Stafford Road.

400TH APPEARANCE

LEN MILLARD, the West Bromwich Albion left-back, passed another milestone in his career with the club last Saturday when he made his 400th appearance in the Albion side. He has missed only a handful of games since the war, and Saturday was his 50th game without a break. To mark the occasion Millard was honoured with the captaincy of the Albion side, and after the game the players autographed the ball used in the match and presented it to him.

Millard, who is 31, has been with Albion since 1937, but it was not until 1942 that he signed professional forms. He made his first appearance in the senior side on August 29, 1942, and has been a first choice for the team ever since.

Millard, who was born at Coseley, began his football career with Christ Church Schools, and later joined Coseley Town in the Wolverhampton League. He then went to Bilston Borough and it was while with them that he signed amateur forms for Albion in 1937.

He has played in every position for Albion except outside-right and goal, but it was generally accepted that his best position was wing-half until, following an injury to Kinsell four seasons ago, he was tried out at left-back. Since then Albion have never had to look further for their left-back. An example of his versatility is that twice, from the centre-forward position, he has scored hat tricks; once was against Wolves and the other against Leicester City. 15.2.52

Bilston Croquet Club, 14th May 1953.

" Buckley Babe "

WOLVERHAMPTON Wanderers have won the Central League hampionship for the third successive year, and after their victory ver Sheffield Wednesday at Iolineux on Monday the trophy as presented to winghalf Bill axter, who has captained the side each of the three championship easons.

Baxter, who is 29, has never succeeded in establishing a regular osition in the Wolves' League side, ut he has been one of their outanding reserves.

He has been on Wolves books for 5 years, being a " Buckley babe " of ne pre-war era. He was first potted by Wolves as a schoolboy of 4 in his native Fifeshire, and was gned as an amateur in the 1938-39 eason. He served in the Navy durng the war, and on his demobilisaon after five years' service he ecame a professional with Wolves. le made his first senior appearance December, 1948, and since then e has been in and out of the eague side. Last season he played 20 League games, and in the eason just ending he has made a air number of appearances.

Baxter is also an accomplished olfer, playing at the Oxley Park lub, Wolverhampton. He won the Iidland qualifying section of the rofessional footballers' golf championship last year, and was among ne leaders in the national competion in the past two years. 1.5.53

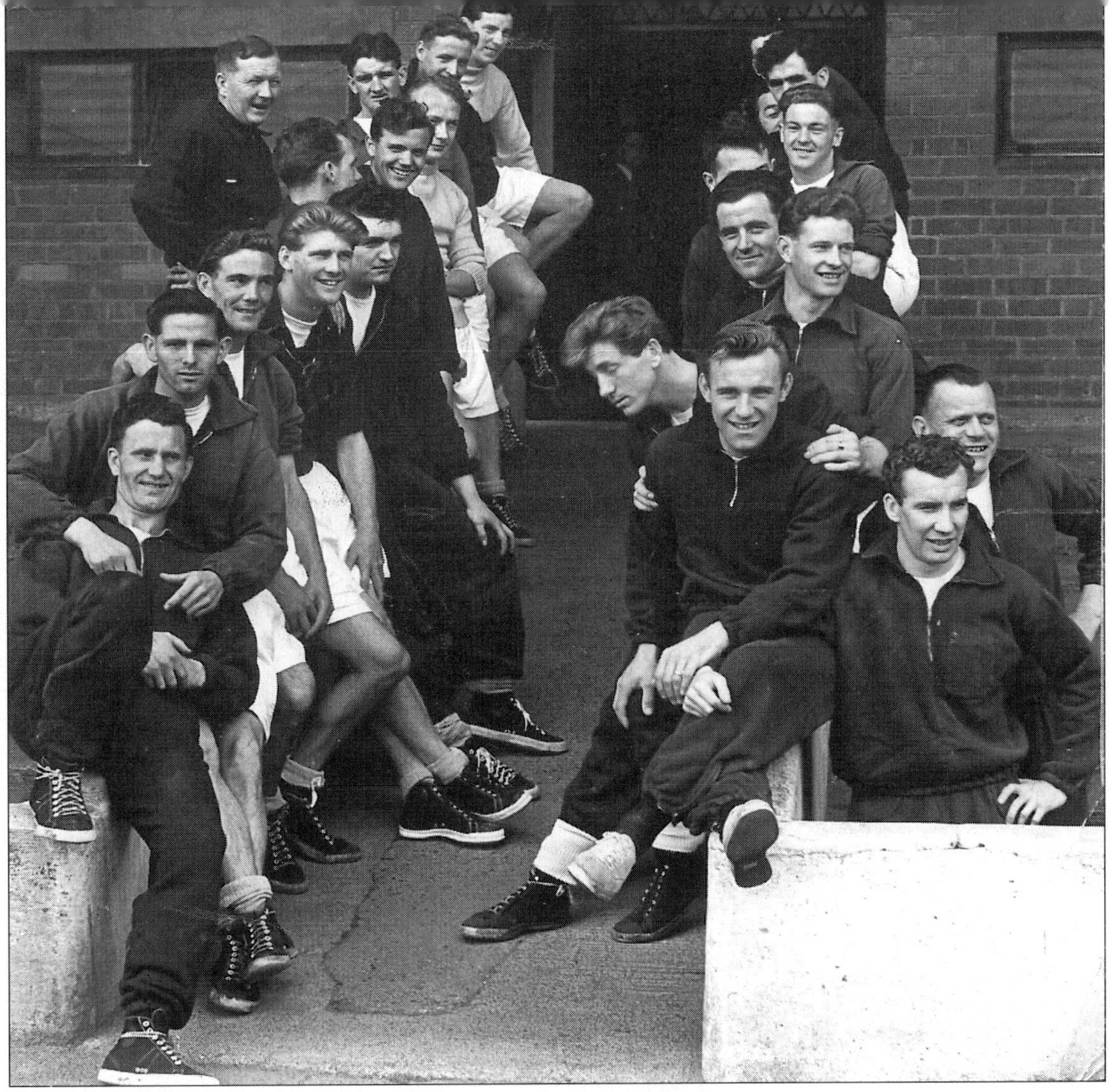

Pre-season training begins for West Bromwich Albion players, 22nd July 1954.

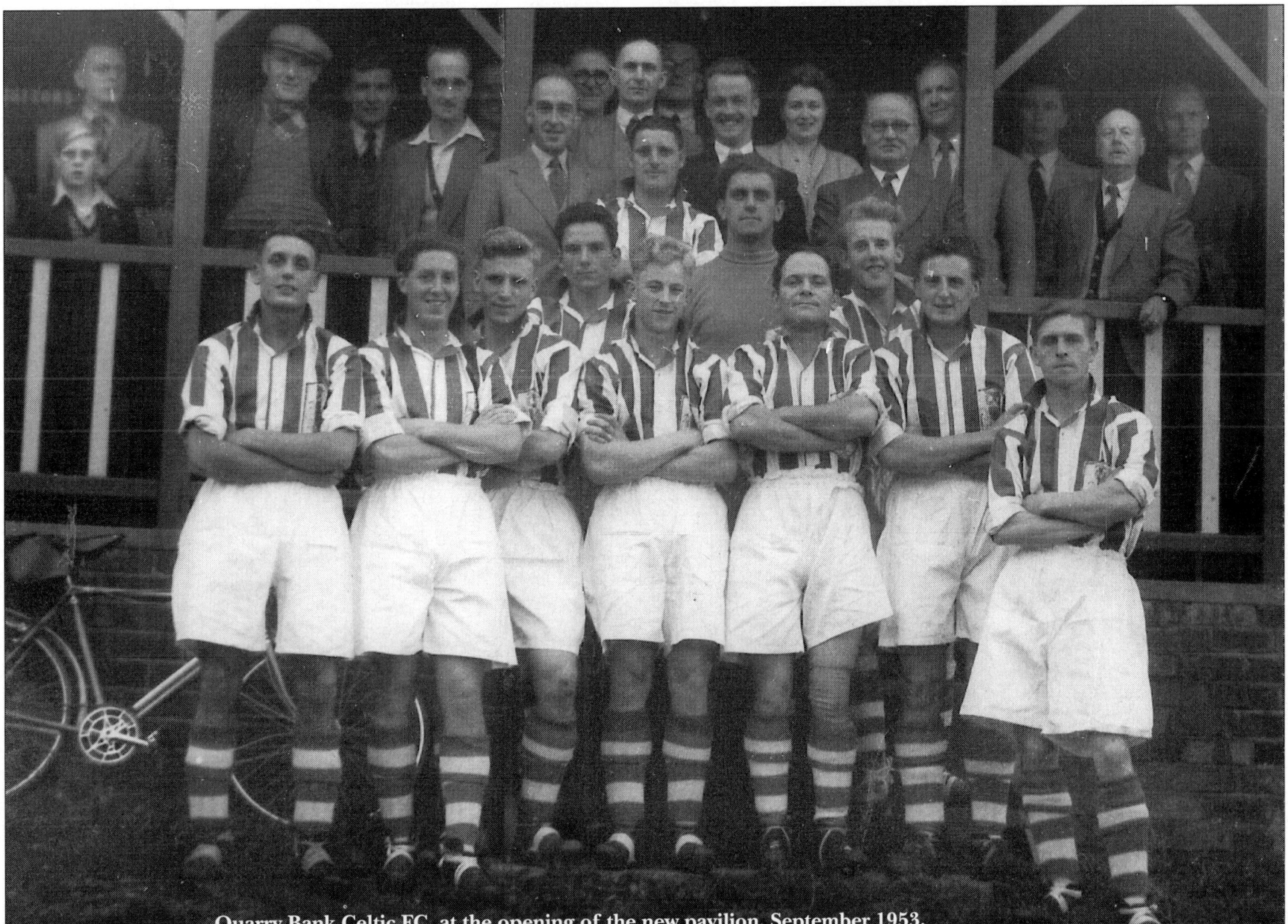

Quarry Bank Celtic FC, at the opening of the new pavilion, September 1953.

Cup Retained by West Bromwich

West Bromwich Harriers, competing on a points basis with Oldbury and Harborne Harriers, yesterday retained the Friendship Cup at Dartmouth Park. The trophy was afterwards presented to W. White, the captain, by the Mayor, Ald. J. D. Davies. Principal results:—

MEN'S EVENTS

100 yards: 1, J. Lowe (West Bromwich); 2, W. Barber (West Bromwich); 3, J. Carr (Oldbury).

880 yards: 1, W. Payne (Oldbury); 2, W. White (West Bromwich); 3, A. Taite (West Bromwich).

220 yards: 1, G. Green (West Bromwich); 2, A. Carr (Oldbury); 3, R. Southall (Oldbury).

440 yards: 1, W. White (West Bromwich); 2, C. Ashmore (West Bromwich); 3, A. Cottrell (Harborne).

Mile team race: 1, West Bromwich; 2, Harborne.

Mile medley relay: 1, West Bromwich; 2, Oldbury; 3, Harborne.

WOMEN'S EVENTS

100 yards: 1, J. Coley (Harborne); 2, I. Sheldon (West Bromwich); 3, V. Owen (West Bromwich).

880 yards: 1, N. Mason (Harborne); 2, A. Withey (Harborne); 3, E. Randle (West Bromwich).

220 yards: 1, J. Coley (Harborne); 2, J. Sharples (Harborne); 3, V. Owen (West Bromwich).

440 yards: 1, H. Ponter (Harborne); 2, C. Holder (West Bromwich).

Relay: 1, Harborne; 2, West Bromwich.

YOUTHS

880 yards: 1, J. Prosser (Harborne); 2, W. Holloway (Oldbury); 3, C. Blogg (West Bromwich).

100 yards: 1, A. Burford (Oldbury); 2, J. Prosser (Harborne); 3, D. Bache (Harborne).

80 yards (girls): 1, P. Moore (West Bromwich); 2, M. Owen (West Bromwich); 3, N. Coley (Harborne).

CYCLING EVENTS

Dartmouth Cycling Club 440 yards scratch: 1, D. W. Richards; 2, J. Jones; 3, C. Waldron.

880 yards handicap: 1, J. Wheatley; 2, D. Waldron; 3, M. Meads.

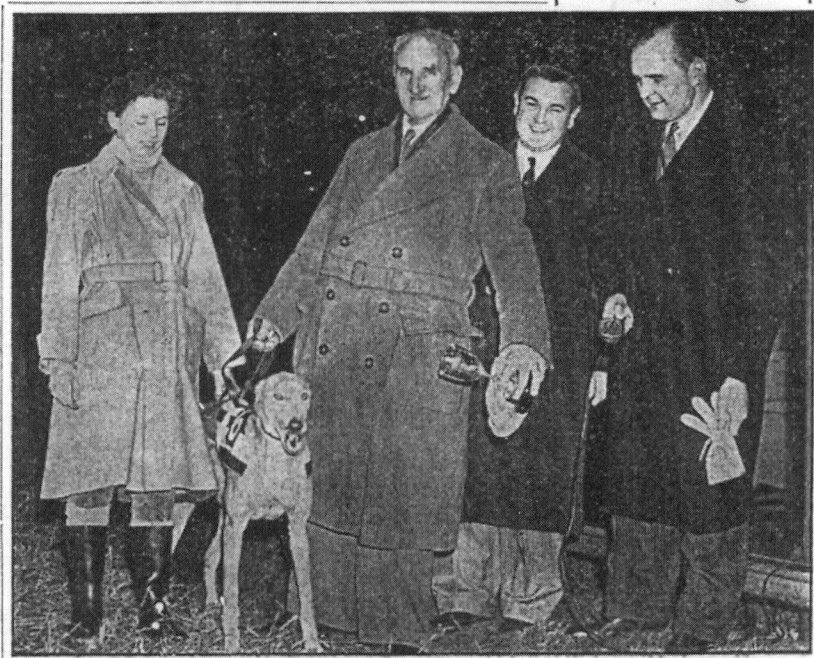

Mr. Bill Horton, of Bloxwich, with the Monmore Green inter-track race trophy winner, Mrs. Horton's dog, Connie Return. The trophy was presented by Mr. R. J. Davies, Sports Editor of "The Birmingham Mail" The event was run in aid of the "Christmas Tree" Fund, the rival tracks, Wolverhampton and King's Heath, each giving £25 to the fund. On the right is Mr. Peter Cartwright, general manager at Monmore Green. The trophy was given by Mr. E. Thomas, the Wolverhampton greyhound owner. 12.12.55

Members of the Halesowen Cycling and Athletic Club, 21st January 1956.

Table Tennis championships, Halesowen, 2nd March 1957.

Charles Forrest, Brierley Hill butcher, happy to display the 15-pounder prize salmon he has landed, 1957.

Small-bore rifle shooting, the Drill Hall, Trindle Road, Dudley, 1954. The Mayor and Mayoress, Coun. and Mrs. Norton can be seen in the background.

Hawbush Youth Club FC, Brierley Hill, 1957.

Swimming Baths, Blowers Green, Dudley, 1957.

Manor Abbey Sports Ground, Manor Lane, Halesowen, 15th June 1957.

Brierley Hill, Sedgley and Tipton Schools' Football Association reception, Brierley Hill Civic Hall, 3rd July 1959.

Walsall Rugby FC, Delves Road, 15th March 1958.

Walsall FC, 1961.

Brierley Hill Bowling League Committee Meeting, 1st March 1958.

Cup presentation, Kingswinford Angling Society, February 1963.

Water ski-ing on Netherton Reservoir, 1963.

The popular Black Country sport of Whippet Racing, Halesowen, 27th April 1963.

Brierley Hill Cricket Club, 13th July 1965.

Duport Sports CC, winners of the Don Kenyon knock-out trophy, 1965.

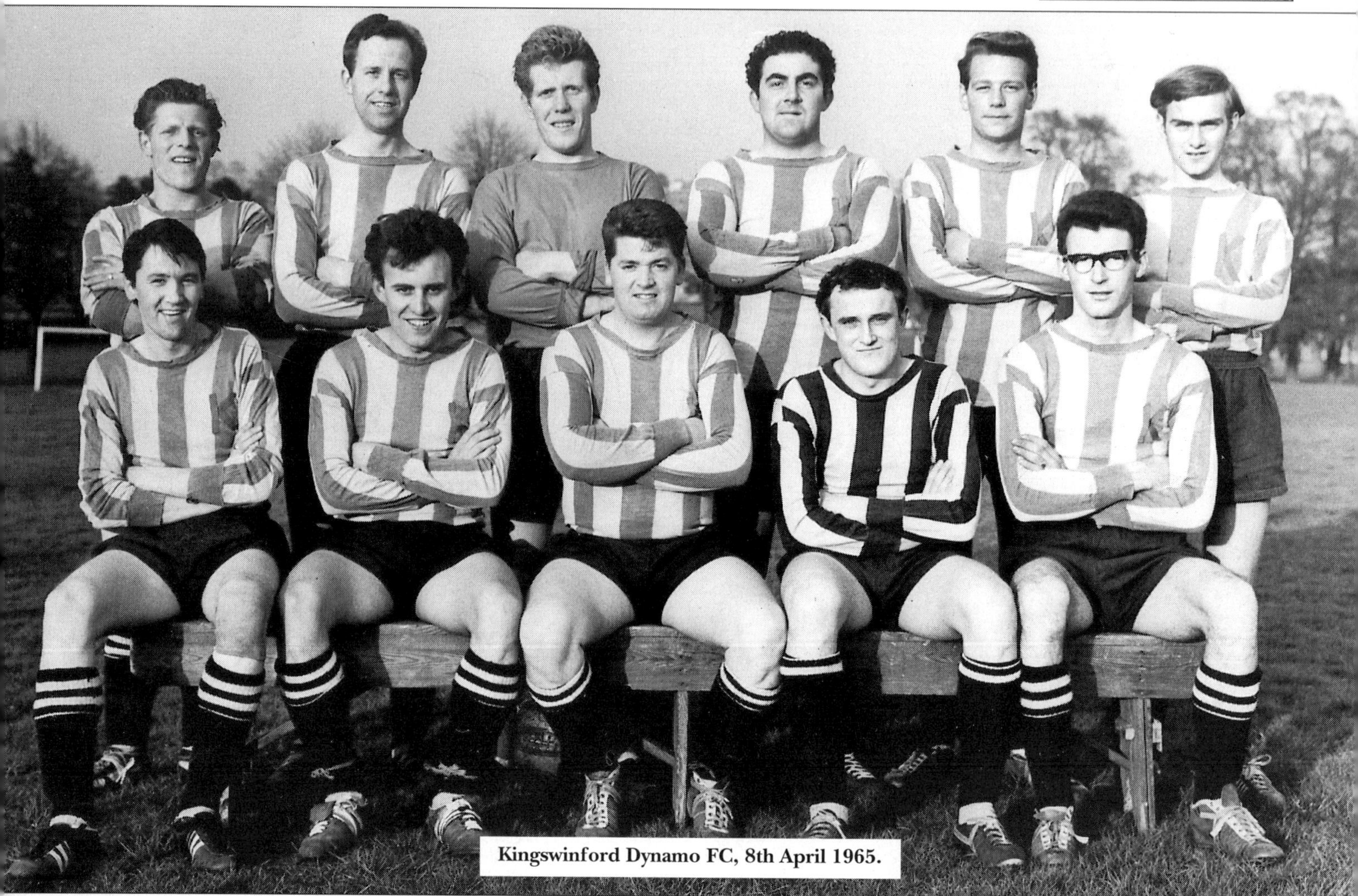

Kingswinford Dynamo FC, 8th April 1965.

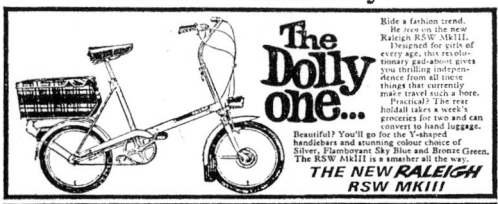

SLAPSTICK LAUNCHES SWIMMING LESSONS

COMMITTEE men dressed in Victorian costume put on a slapstick comedy to launch lessons for physically handicapped people at Bloxwich Baths.

Mr. Geoff Walker, Chairman of the Walsall and District Physically Handicapped Association, took part in the show and later described the swimming tuition as "one of the most worthwhile things we have ever done."

Long distance swimmer Mr. Bill Pickering, Superintendent of Bloxwich Baths, helped about 20 physically handicapped people learning to swim. He said that another 10 had decided to join in next week. 14.4.70

54

WEST BROMWICH RAMBLERS 10.12.71

THERE was a good turnout for Sunday's ramble to Cannock Chase and 33 members travelled to Broadhurst Green by car.

The ramble started from the German Military Cemetery there and, led by Bill Perry, the ramblers walked down the beautiful Sherbrook Valley past the Sherbrook pools.

After a break for elevenses at Marquis's Drive they continued through Haywood Slade and joined the Nature Trail near Seven Springs, which took them to the Stepping Stones. From there it was a short walk over Oat Hill to Milford Common where lunch was taken.

The afternoon's walk was through Brocton Coppice and along the top of the hills to the Glacier Stone, which was deposited on the Chase during the last ice-age, from its original home in the Southern Uplands of Scotland.

The party returned to Broadhurst Green by way of Brocton Field, Pepper Slade and Parr's Warren having covered about 10 miles on a very mild December day.

The club's next ramble will be the Christmas dinner and ramble to the Lenchford near Shrawley and will complete the club's programme for this year. The programme for the first six months of next year is being prepared and anyone interested in joining can obtain one by writing to the Secretary, c/o West Bromwich Community Centre, Gayton Road, West Bromwich.

World Centenary of Cycle Racing
1868—1968

West Smethwick Park

on Wednesday 5th June '68

7.00 p.m. **Programme 6d**

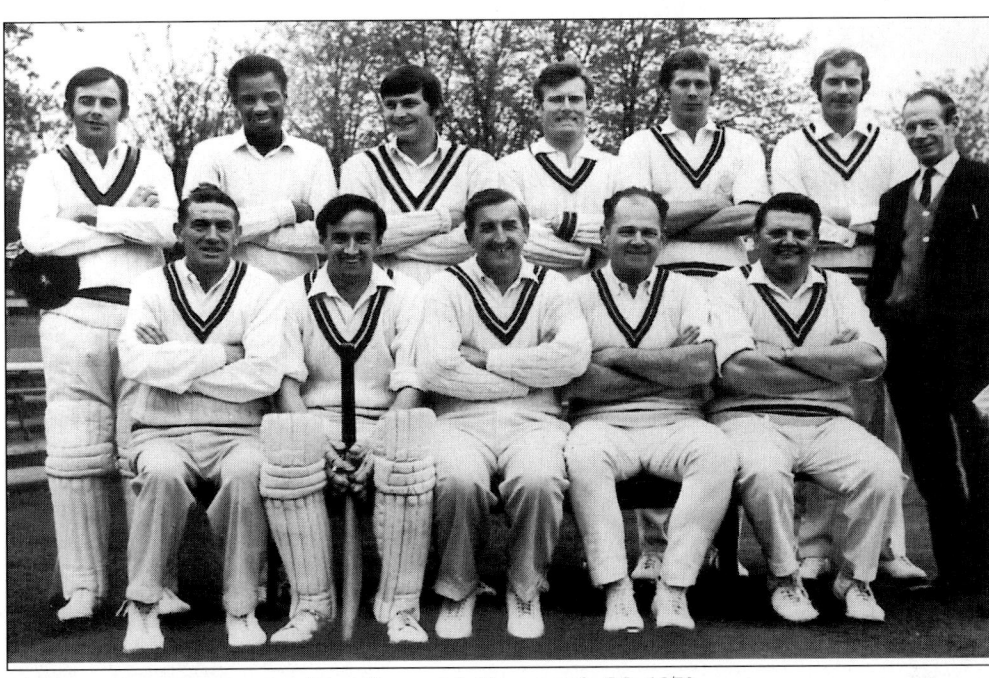

West Bromwich Dartmouth CC, 1970.

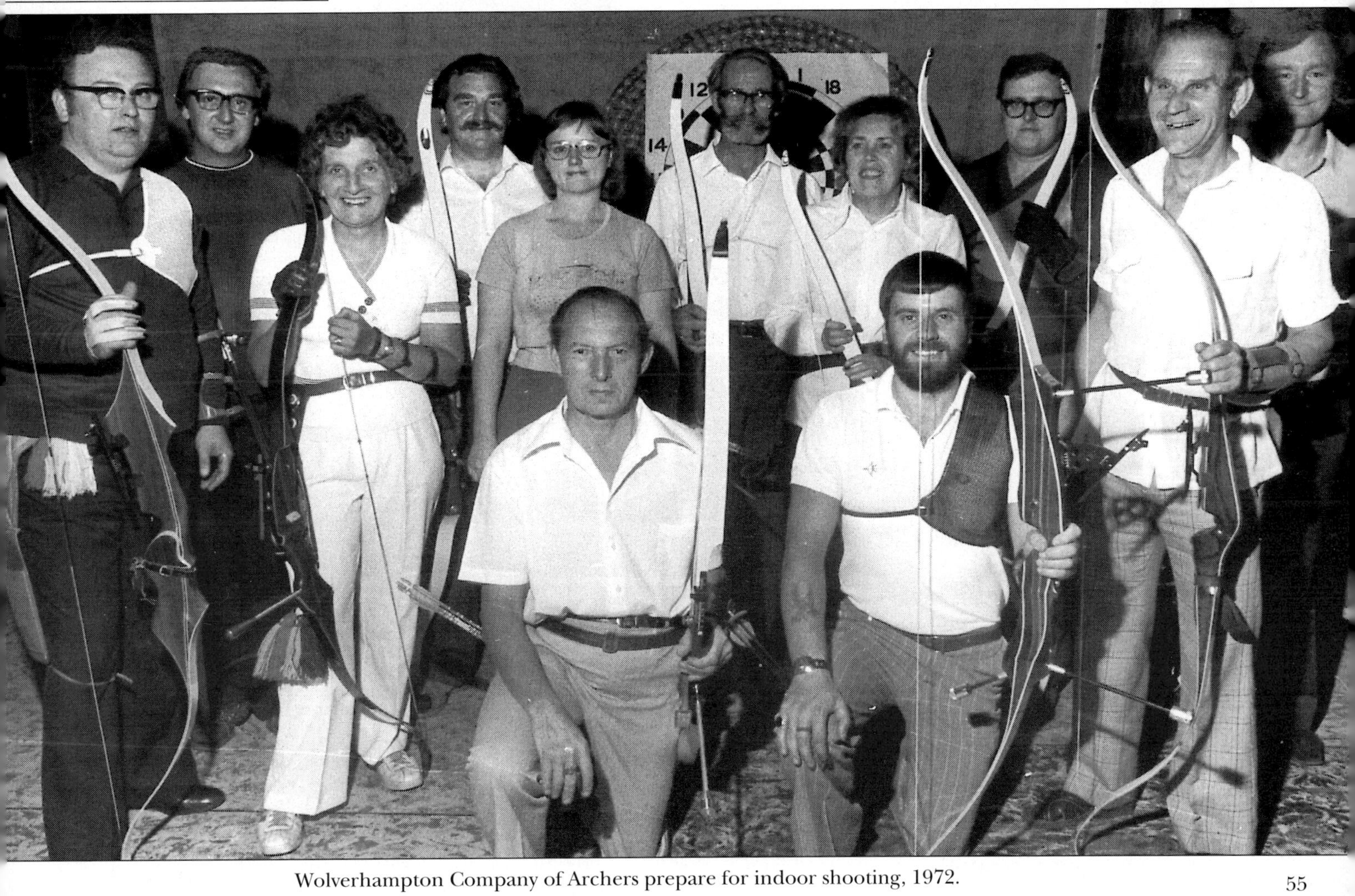

Wolverhampton Company of Archers prepare for indoor shooting, 1972.

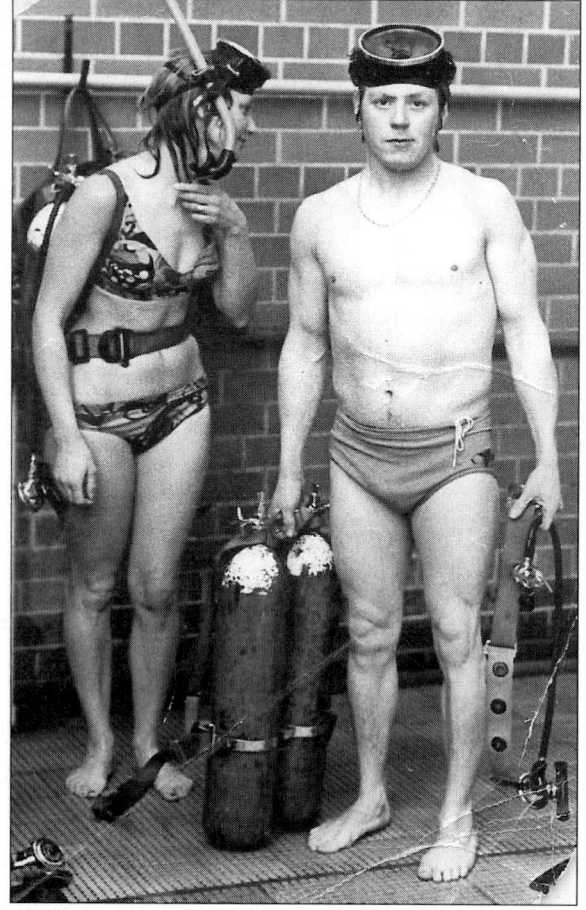

Margaret Higgins and Bob Mortimer, of the Warley Underwater Diving Club, prepare to take the plunge, Langley Baths, 1973. The club is now known as the Warley Divers.

Great Pool, Himley Hall, Dudley, 1972.

10.12.71

JUNE PITCHFORD, of Old-bury and District Cycling Club, took her place among the country's top time trialists on Saturday evening at the British best all-rounder competition dinner-dance and prize presentation at London.

At the prize presentation, awards were made to the 12 fastest men and the six fastest women riders, based on their performances over the past season.

June received a certificate for taking fourth place in the women's competition with an average speed of 23.760 m.p.h. over distances of 25, 50 and 100 miles.

She was also awarded a silver medal for second place in the women's national 100, when she recorded 4hrs. 26min. 1sec.

June. who lives at Romsley, attended the presentation with her husband and trainer, Ken, himself a former racing man.

30.5.73
Trophy for Kingswinford

Dudley Kingswinford won their own annual Spring Bank Holiday six-a-side cricket tournament for the first time.

Kingswinford second team took the trophy by beating Old Halesonians, twice previous winners, in the final.

Halesonians scored 36 in their allotted five overs and Kingswinford won with an over to spare.

10.3.75

GOLDEN - GIRL Verona Elder is now the unchallenged queen of European indoor 400-metres running. She proved her right to the crown with a runaway win in the European Indoor Championships at Katowice.

The Wolverhampton and Bilston girl raced home in a new United Kingdom women's 400m. indoor best time of 52.68 seconds.

In second place was Russia's European record holder Nadezdha Ilvina.

THE Nelson from Halesowen are through to the quarter-finals of the Sports Argus Inn-Quiz competition, which is sponsored by Mitchells and Butlers Ltd.

And they made it by three seconds. In their replayed tie-breaker question against the Dugdale Arms from Nuneaton they answered the question correctly in 57 seconds.

The Dugdale did it in exactly one minute.

MAY 1975

Sandwell's Dennis Burton opens the first frame against Walsall in the Black Country Olympics' Snooker Tournament, Smethwick Ex-Servicemen's Club, 25th April 1976.

Walsall Football Club playing staff, 5th July 1976.

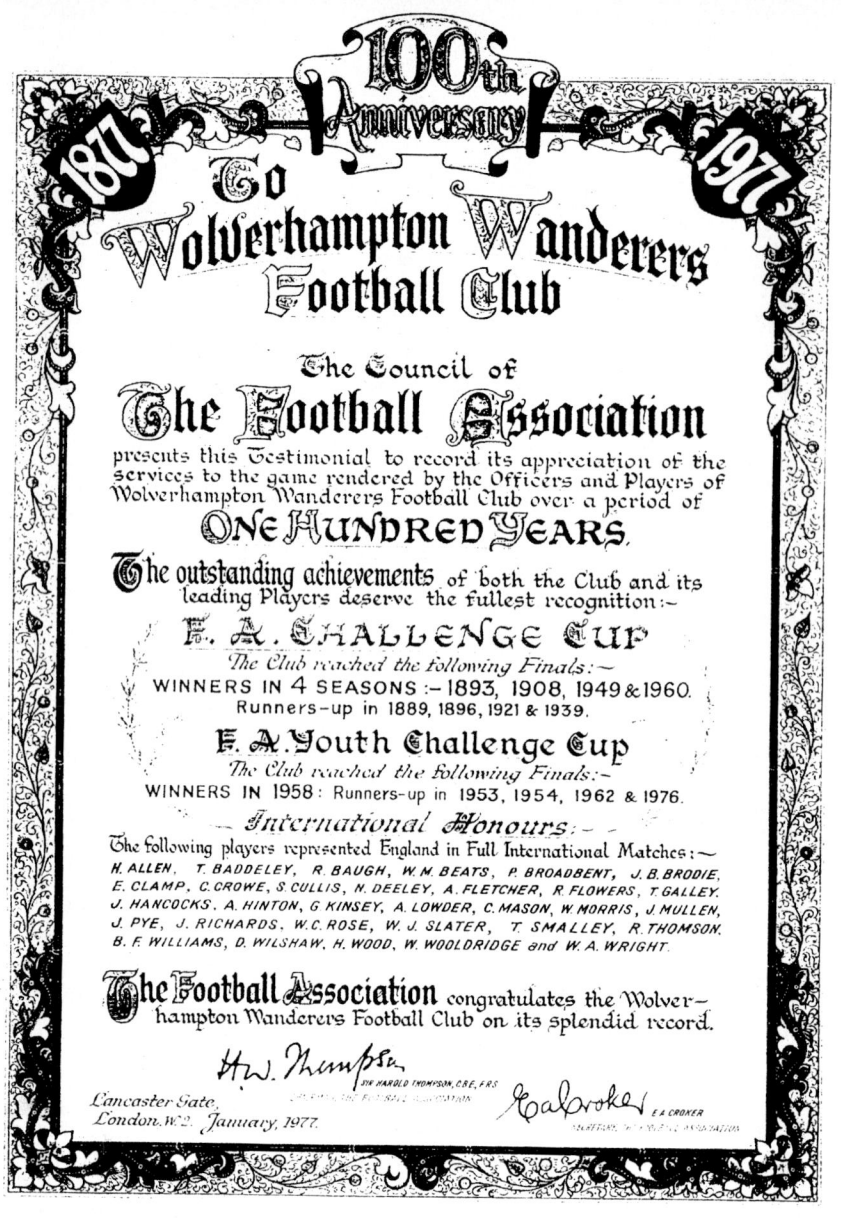

100th Anniversary 1877–1977

To
**Wolverhampton Wanderers
Football Club**

The Council of
The Football Association

presents this Testimonial to record its appreciation of the services to the game rendered by the Officers and Players of Wolverhampton Wanderers Football Club over a period of

ONE HUNDRED YEARS.

The outstanding achievements of both the Club and its leading Players deserve the fullest recognition:—

F. A. CHALLENGE CUP

The Club reached the following Finals:—
WINNERS IN 4 SEASONS:— 1893, 1908, 1949 & 1960.
Runners-up in 1889, 1896, 1921 & 1939.

F. A. Youth Challenge Cup

The Club reached the following Finals:—
WINNERS IN 1958: Runners-up in 1953, 1954, 1962 & 1976.

International Honours

The following players represented England in Full International Matches:—
H. ALLEN, T. BADDELEY, R. BAUGH, W. M. BEATS, P. BROADBENT, J. B. BRODIE, E. CLAMP, C. CROWE, S. CULLIS, N. DEELEY, A. FLETCHER, R. FLOWERS, T. GALLEY, J. HANCOCKS, A. HINTON, G. KINSEY, A. LOWDER, C. MASON, W. MORRIS, J. MULLEN, J. PYE, J. RICHARDS, W. C. ROSE, W. J. SLATER, T. SMALLEY, R. THOMSON, B. F. WILLIAMS, D. WILSHAW, H. WOOD, W. WOOLDRIDGE and W. A. WRIGHT.

The Football Association congratulates the Wolverhampton Wanderers Football Club on its splendid record.

H. W. Thompson
Sir Harold Thompson, C.B.E., F.R.S.

E. A. Croker
E. A. Croker

Lancaster Gate,
London, W.2. January, 1977.

Darlaston hit their top form

8.3.75

In the Midland BASKETBALL first division, Darlaston, relegated from the Premier group last year, hit top form to beat Old Marts 72-70.

Dargan (20) gave Darlaston a good start to the match but they allowed themselves to be rattled by an Old Marts revival. Finally it was left to Lycett (10), with two free shots in the last seconds of play, to secure the win for Darlaston.

Bournville were completely outclassed by Alsager going down by 29-55.

In the second division, Ada Road made all the early running against Stanmore and with 10 minutes left, led 65-45. Then Ada Road stars Rowlands and Tolley fouled out, leaving the way clear for Wilkes (33) and Edwards (14) to shoot Stanmore to a 75-72 win.

In division three, Cosford fought back bravely against Stoke to tie the match 50-50 at full-time with two baskets in the last minute. The extra period, however, went all Stoke's way with a 56-52 scoreline.

West Bromwich continued their strong bid for promotion as Roberts hit 23 points to inspire them to a 74-32 thrashing of Birmingham University. Bromsgrove also left themselves well placed after a 60-42 win over Bushbury.

Wolverhampton Wanderers and England football captain, Billy Wright. A director of Wolves and the former Head of Sport at Central T.V.

Tettenhall's Rachel Heyhoe-Flint, former -England's Women's Cricket Captain.

Wolverhampton Football Referee, Jack Taylor, an ex-master butcher.

Folk Group "Giggetty" entertain the Dudley 'It's a Knockout' squad, during their training for the BBC TV competition, 1979.

Wolverhampton Wanderers players celebrate winning The Football League Cup, 15th March 1980.

Victory parade! Wolverhampton Wanderers bring home The Football League Cup, Sunday, 16th March 1980.

The victorious Wednesbury Labour Club darts squad, after winning the Victory League championship, 9th December 1977.

Dudley Leisure Centre, Wellington Road, 1982.

Teams in the northern area of the Brierley Hill and Dudley Schools FA are presented with a new cup by the TSB Group. Bank Manager, Dennis Moore, hands the cup to Ivan Southall, Chairman of the Schools FA, 12th March 1980.

Wednesbury British Legion team proudly display their West Bromwich Works' Snooker League trophy, 25th March 1980.

West Bromwich Albion playing staff line-up for the new season, 5th August 1983.

Paul Chaplin, Sandwell Mail Circulation Manager, presents Terry Turner with the Free Press Challenge Cup after The George Pub, of Oldbury, won the bowls competition, by beating Michells and Butlers in the final, 4th September 1983.

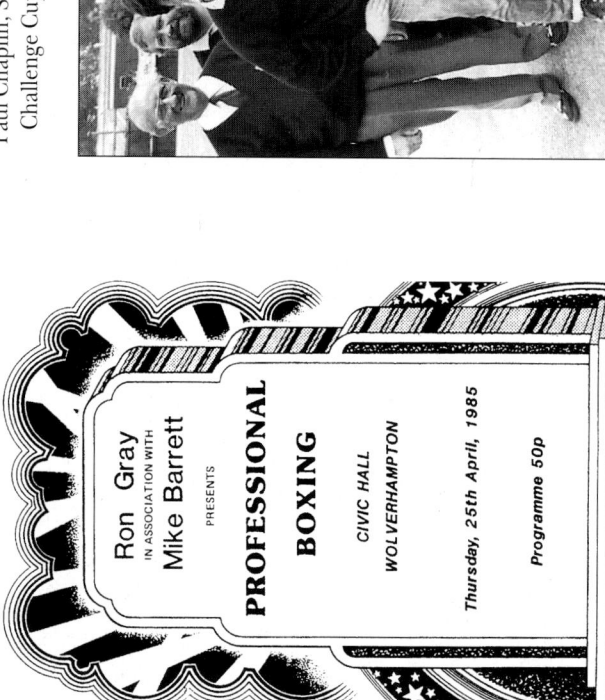

Ron Gray
IN ASSOCIATION WITH
Mike Barrett
PRESENTS

PROFESSIONAL BOXING

CIVIC HALL
WOLVERHAMPTON

Thursday, 25th April, 1985

Programme 50p

Jackie Westley tries out the new leisure route along West Bromwich Parkway, 8th April 1983.

England hockey player, Neil Mallett, coaches youngsters from the West Park Sixth Form College, Smethwick, at Hadley Stadium, 10th December 1987.

Sir Jack Hayward, OBE, who became President of Wolverhampton Wanderers in 1986.

Ron Atkinson after signing a one-year contract as Manager of West Bromwich Albion, 3rd September 1987.

The Ringway Fitness Centre, West Bromwich, 13th November 1986.

National Cycle Festival, Market Place, Dudley, 1988.

Walsall CC, 1990.

A team from the Bull's Head, Sedgley, aboard their raft "Banana Split", take part in the annual charity race, River Severn, Bridgnorth, June 1992. The pub celebrated its 200th birthday in 1994.

RON GRAY & PAT COWDELL
PROUDLY PRESENT

PROFESSIONAL BOXING
WALSALL TOWN HALL

DOORS OPEN 7.00 p.m

MONDAY 18th APRIL 1994

COMMENCE 8.00 p.m.

ACTION PACKED TOURNAMENT FEATURING

PETER TILL
(WALSALL) British Champion this Year ?

versus

KARL TAYLOR
(BIRMINGHAM)

NIGEL RAFFERTY
(WOLVERHAMPTON)

versus

LEE ARCHER
(DUDLEY)

SPONSORED BY

Leamore Windows ltd.
(0922) 473737

HOWARD 'CLAKA' CLARKE
(WARLEY)

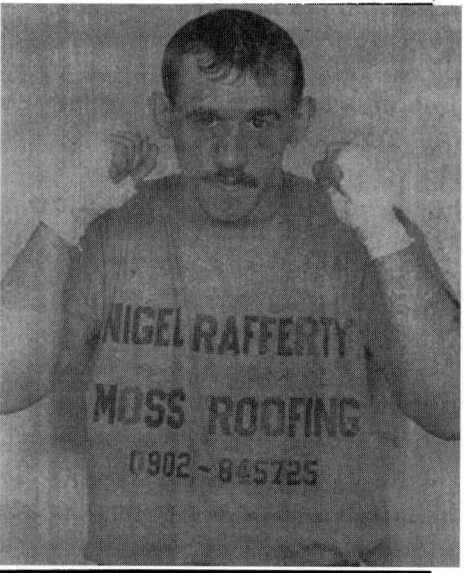

KARL SMALLWOOD
(ATHERSTONE)

PATRICK PARTON
(TELFORD)

TICKETS: £20 Ringside : £15 : £10 Limited Number

Tickets in advance from Ron Gray 0543 502049; Ken Rushton 021 559 9117; Walsall Town Hall 0922 650600; Pat Cowdell 021 552 8082; Peter Till 0922 39318;
Gary Osborne 0922 712834; Howard Clarke, Arthur Smallwood 0827 715860; Nigel Rafferty 0831 410707; Mossa 0902 845725;
Ted Rafferty, 13 Shelley Road, Fordhouses, Wolverhampton 0922 496467

THAT'S ENTERTAINMENT

Essington Village Band, c. 1900.

SCOTCH WHISKY   M. & B.

"DUMBARTON"

M. & B.   THOROUGHLY MATURED

68

Entertaining audiences all around the Black Country, Aldridge Colliery Silver Prize Band, 1925.

The Picture House, Bridge Street, Walsall, c. 1927.

The Olympia, Brierley Hill Road, Wordsley, c. 1922. It
was part of a brewery, converted to a cinema in 1912.
Known locally and affectionately as "The Limp".

YOU'LL ENJOY THESE FAMOUS MUSICAL COMEDY AIRS OF THIRTY YEARS AGO!

Columbia New Process RECORDS 4/6

DEBROY SOMERS BAND

12-inch Dark Blue Label. 4/6 Each.

9881 LIONEL MONCKTON MEMORIES (*Lionel Monckton*). In Two Parts
Introducing: Part 1.—Keep Off the Grass (The Toreador); The Rajah of Bhong (The Country Girl); Under the Deodar (The Country Girl); Peace (The Country Girl). Part 2—Arcady is Ever Young (The Arcadians); The Pipes of Pan (The Arcadians); My Cinnamon Tree (The Cingalee); Come to the Ball (The Quaker Girl); The Soldiers in the Park (The Runaway Girl).

9882 IVAN CARYLL MEMORIES (*Ivan Caryll*)—
Introducing: From Far Peru (The Orchid); By the Shores of the Mediterranean (The Earl and the Girl); Espana (The Toreador); The Toreador's Song (The Toreador); Beautiful Lady (The Pink Lady).
PAUL RUBENS MEMORIES (*Paul Rubens*)—
Introducing: Soldiers of the Netherlands (Miss Hook of Holland); Sleepy Canal (Miss Hook of Holland); She Was a Miller's Daughter (Three Little Maids); Sloe Eyes (The Cingalee); Here's to Love (The Sunshine Girl).

HAPPY memories of a bygone generation! Lionel Monckton was one of a brilliant coterie who wrote special songs for the Gaiety productions of a quarter of a century ago, afterwards writing full-length comedies, such as "The Arcadians," for Dalys. Ivan Caryll was a Belgian who contributed, like Monckton, many catchy songs towards light operettas; and Paul Rubens (whose "Cingalee" was written in conjunction with Lionel Monckton) was another of the brilliant English school who helped keep London much gayer and brighter than it is now.

1929

Columbia New Process RECORDS

For Best Service, Hear the New Columbia Records at the Columbia Specialists . . . . . Biggest Choice

UNITED TALKING MACHINES CO. LTD.

6, PRINCE'S SQUARE
WOLVERHAMPTON
AND AT HALL ST., DUDLEY
Phone 1870

NO SCRATCH NO SCRATCH

WOOD'S PALACE, BILSTON

TO-NIGHT. FRANKIE DARRO in "CIRCUS KID" TO-NIGHT.
Also RIN-TIN-TIN in "LAND OF THE SILVER FOX."
ALL NEXT WEEK, 6.0 to 10.30; MATINEES MONDAY, THURSDAY, and SATURDAY, at 2.30:

GREAT ALL TALKING SENSATION
"ON TRIAL"
Starring PAULINE FREDERICK

1929

The Cosy Cinema SAVOY High St., Bilston

TO-NIGHT. MAY McAVOY & CONRAD NAGEL in "CAUGHT IN THE FOG." 6.0 10.30.
On the Stage: Surprising Spectacular Novelty, TACETO, who paints without paint.
NEXT MONDAY, TUESDAY, AND WEDNESDAY.

ON THE SCREEN: WARNER BAXTER in "DANGER STREET"
ON THE STAGE: Great Vocal, Dancing, & Electric Novelty by MACK and DAISY
THURS. NEXT: Jack London's "SMOKE BELLEW," & New Serial by Edgar Wallace.

PALACE, OLD SQUARE, WALSALL

MONDAY NEXT, OCTOBER 14th, FOR ONE WEEK ONLY.
"SWEENEY TODD"
THE DEMON BARBER OF FLEET STREET.
"WEEK-END WIVES"
A SCREAMING LAUGHTER-PROVOKING COMEDY DRAMA.
See Premier Silents in a Musical Atmosphere.

GROSVENOR CINEMA, BLOXWICH

THE HOME OF SUPER FILMS!
WEEK COMMENCING MONDAY NEXT, OCTOBER 14th.
MONDAY, TUESDAY, AND WEDNESDAY: HENRY EDWARDS in "FEAR"
Supported by HOLMES HERBERT in "THROUGH THE BREAKERS."
THURSDAY, FRIDAY, AND SATURDAY: LILLIAN HALL-DAVIS, HENRY VICTOR in "TOMMY ATKINS"
Also FRED THOMSON in "KIT CARSON."

"COME TO THE FAIR!"
"WHAT FAIR?"
"THE ORANGE TREE FAIR."
IN THE
MUNICIPAL BATHS ASSEMBLY ROOMS
OCTOBER 29th, 30th, and 31st.
BUY ATTRACTIVE HANDBOOK,
Three Days' Admission for 6d.

DANCING.
ST. PETER'S INSTITUTE,
EVERY SATURDAY, 7.30 to 11 p.m.
ADMISSION ONE SHILLING.
Spot Prizes Worth Winning.
"NIGHT LIGHTS" BAND.

LILLESHALL ILLUMINATIONS.
THE BEAUTIFUL GARDENS ILLUMINATED NIGHTLY from dusk till 10 p.m.
Music and Dancing.
ADMISSION after 6.30, 6d.

NATIONAL UNION DISTRIBUTIVE AND ALLIED WORKERS
Wolverhampton Branch.
WHIST DRIVE AND DANCE.
CO-OPERATIVE HALL, STAFFORD ST.,
MONDAY NEXT, OCTOBER 14th,
At 7.30. Good Prizes.
BURLINGTON DANCE ORCHESTRA.
Whist & Dance inclusive 1s. Dance Only 6d.
Dancing 10 till 12.

MISS ALLEN'S FIRST AFTER-DINNER DANCE
WILL BE HELD AT THE
VICTORIA HOTEL ON OCTOBER 19th.
8.30 to 11.30. Tickets 4s. 6d.
ROBERT THOMAS AND HIS BAND.
Tables may be booked in the Ballroom, and Light Dinners from 3s. 6d. may be had in the Hotel.

WHY NOT JOIN
MISS DOROTHY MAY'S DANCING CLASSES?
28, DARLINGTON ST., WOLVERHAMPTON.
THE NEXT DANCE, Star and Garter Hotel, is on OCTOBER 28th.

Odeon Cinema, Brierley Hill, 14th March 1936.

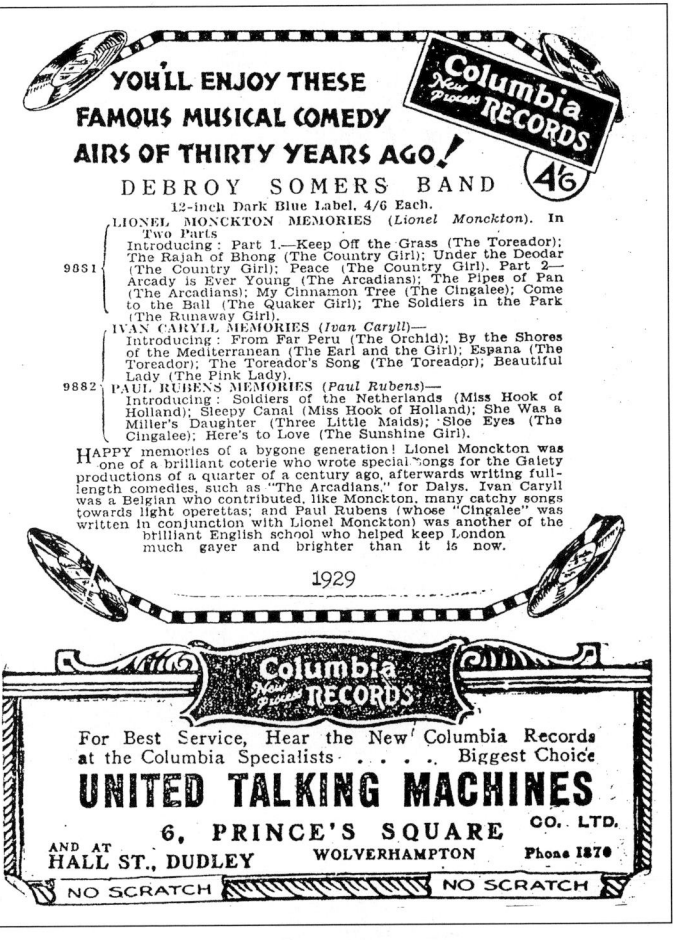

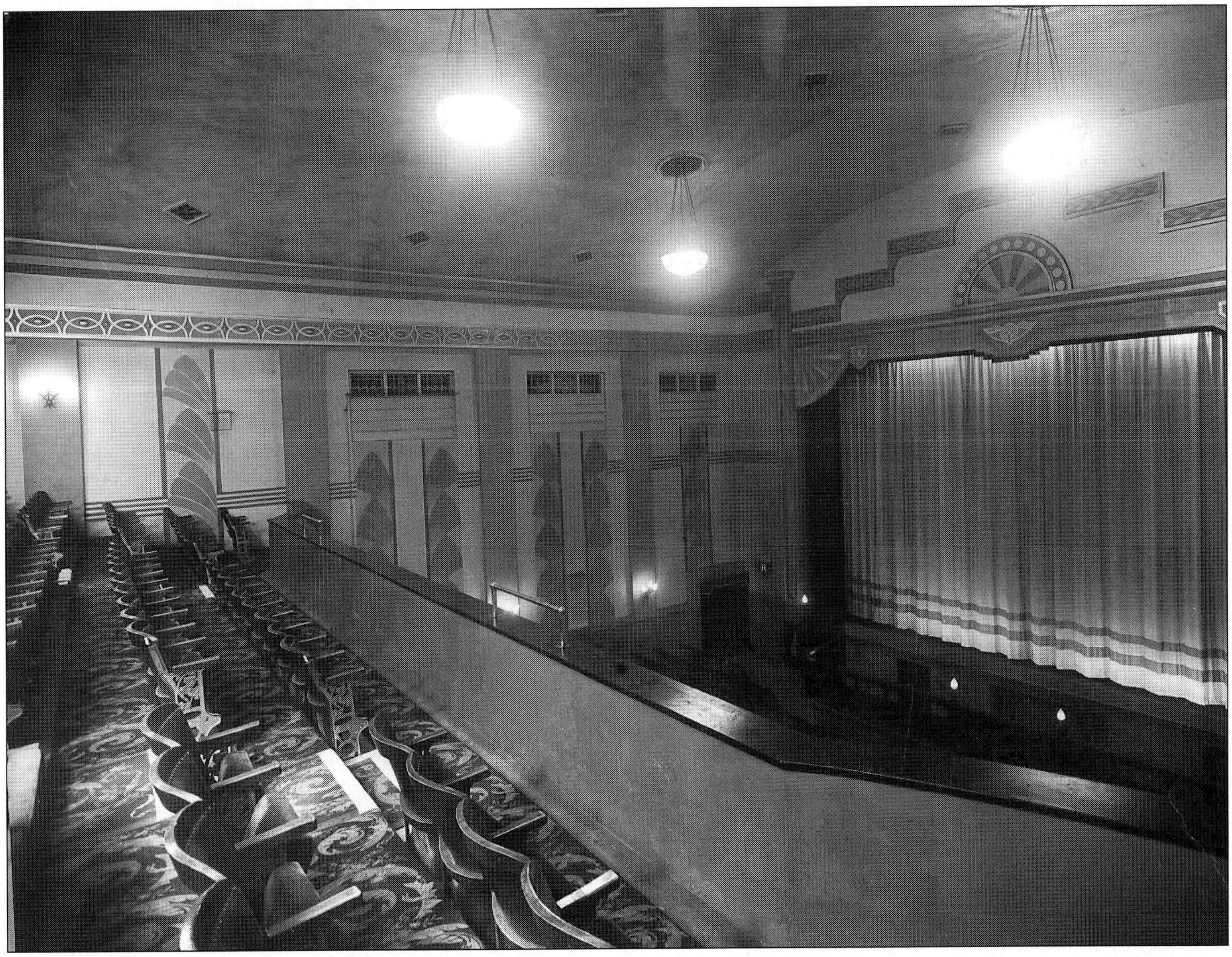

Her Majesty's.

1935

Next week The Walsall Players are presenting "The Good Companions" (by J. B. Priestley), reference to which is made in another column

The Imperial Picture House.

Mae West, the most discussed film star of recent years, can be seen at the Imperial all next week in one of her latest successes, "Belle of the Nineties," which will be screened daily at 3.39, 6.28 and 9.17. Besides starring in the picture, Miss West was the author and scenarist, and the entertaining resultant picture speaks highly of her ability both as actress and writer. She has, as an American beauty of the nineties, a role peculiarly suited to her style. In the story she becomes involved with a young prize-fighter, but through the plotting of the fighter's manager, leaves the town and becomes queen of a gambling resort of New Orleans. The men of the great southern city welcome her in their midst, and the gambling house becomes the town's most popular resort. The further development of the story introduces the prize-fighter again, when he is required to rob his former lady friend. From this point the story moves on to a thrilling climax. The supporting picture all the week will be " Get Your Man," a diverting British-produced comedy with Dorothy Boyd and Clifford Heatherley in the leads. The story tells of a rich young girl who suddenly finds herself in the papers as an advertisement for toothpaste! This leads to complications and romance.

DUDLEY & DISTRICT AMUSEMENTS

PLAZA CINEMA, CASTLE HILL, DUDLEY
'Phone: Dudley 2739.
THE HOUSTON SISTERS in
" THE HAPPY DAYS ARE HERE AGAIN " (U).
Also :
" TO CATCH A THIEF " (A).
Next Week: "Forget Me Not," with Gigli, the famous tenor.

10.12.36

WEST BROMWICH AMUSEMENTS

THEATRE ROYAL, WEST BROMWICH. Phone: 0191 West Bromwich.
ONCE NIGHTLY at 7.15 p.m. Doors open 6.45 p.m.
The West Bromwich Operatic Society present
" THE ARCADIANS."
Full Cast of 60 — Augmented Orchestra.
Proceeds in aid of Local Charities.
PRICES OF ADMISSION (including Tax): Stalls and Dress Circle, 3s.; Side Circle, 2s.; Back Circle, 1s.; Pit, 1s. 6d.; Gallery, 6d.

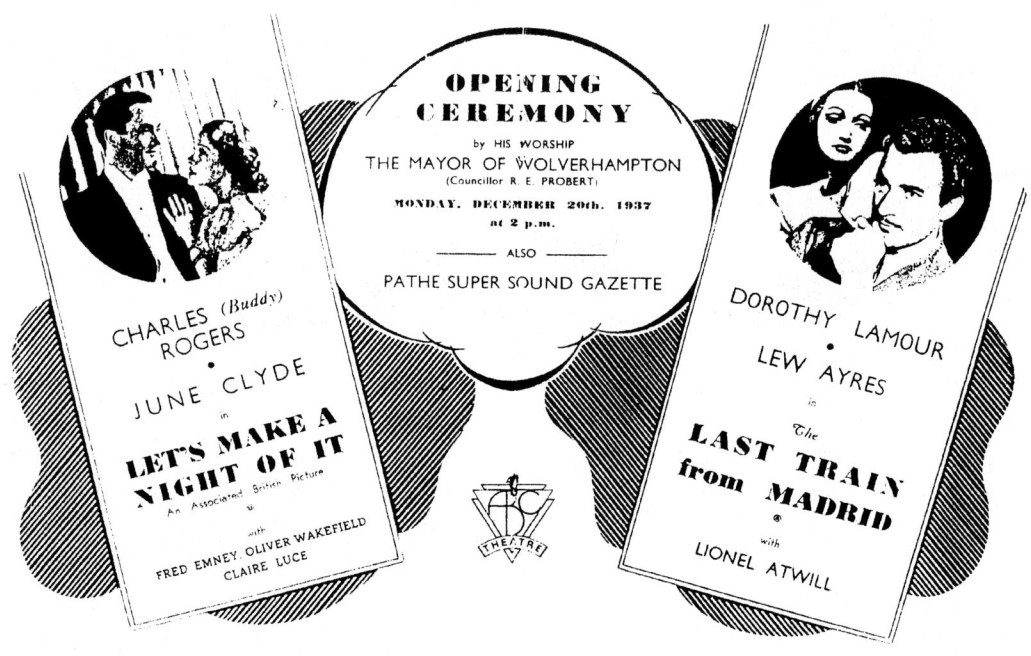

NEW CINEMA OPENED AT WOLVERHAMPTON

21.12.37

The Savoy Cinema, Garrick Street, Wolverhampton, erected by the Associated British Picture Corporation, Ltd., was formally opened by the Mayor yesterday.

The site was originally purchased from the Corporation by the late Mr. Leon Salberg for £10,000, and is in the centre of the town, near two other cinemas, the New Theatre Royal and the Gaumont Palace.

The Savoy is an imposing building, which embodies the latest principles in cinema design, and has street frontages on three sides. On the other is a car park. There is accommodation for 1,800 people, of whom 620 can be seated in the circle.

Mr. W. R. Glenn, the company's architect, was responsible for the design and the general contractors were W. H. Jones and Son, Coventry.

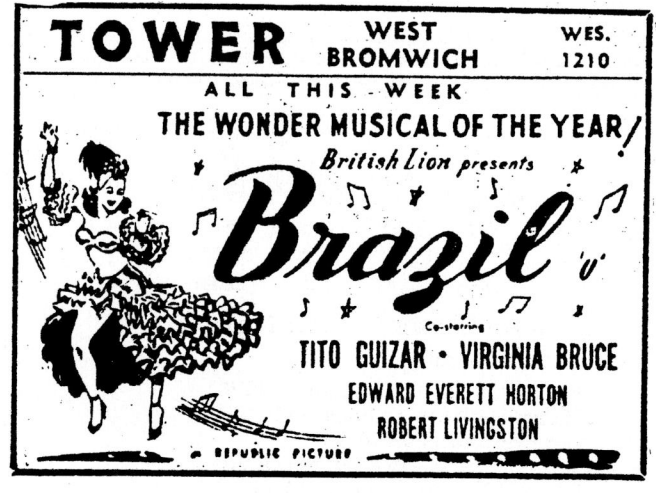

Bing Crosby appearing in "Rhythm on the Range" at Her Majesty's, Walsall.

Her Majesty's Theatre, Town End Bank, Walsall, 1937.

Now for a real HOME CINEMA at very little cost

O.K. for Sound

A PROFESSIONALLY-MADE HOME CINEMA by Pathescope that puts realism into Home Movies. Just what the party needs in up-to-date fun. And you can buy one from as low as 37/6 that will give you brilliant and faithful quality.

Pathéscope, too, bring you the pick of the films—Charlie Chaplin and Harold Lloyd Comedies, Mickey Mouse, Felix and Popeye Cartoons, splendid Dramas—including Classics such as *The Informer* and *The White Hell of Pitz Palu*, Cherry Kearton Animal Comedies, Wild Wests, and even Silly Symphony excerpts —all non-inflammable.

And now for the biggest thrill of all—HOME TALKIES! At last at a reasonable price, nearly half the cost of any Projector of comparable performance. You can *look* and *listen* to Edmund Gwenn, Popeye and great Stars in your own Lounge. Send the Coupon below and find out all about it.

PATHÉ SCOPE

Pioneers in Home Cinematography

AVAILABLE PROJECTORS :

" Ace " Silent Projector	**37/6**
Model 'H' Home Cinema £10.10.0 Dual 9.5 mm. and 16 mm. Projector	**£21.0.0**
" Vox " Sound Projector	**£60.0.0**
Films - - - - from	**3/6**

Today's Radio

14.8.45

HOME London 342; Midland 296; North 449 - 285; West 514 - 203; Scotland 391; Wales 373; N. Ireland 285

6.30 a.m. — Gramophone Records.
7.0 — News. Weather Forecast.
7.20 — The Daily Dozen.
7.35 — Verdi (Records).
7.55 — Lift Up Your Hearts!
8.0 — News. Weather Forecast.
8.20 — The Kitchen Front
8.25 — John Reynders And His Orchestra.
9.0 — Gramophone Records.
9.50 — Albert Sandler Trio.
10.15 — The Daily Service.
10.30 — Music While You Work.
11.0 — Drifting And Dreaming.
11.30 — Orchestras Of The World.
12.10 p.m. — Light Music For Two Pianos.
12.30 — Workers' Playtime.
1.0 — News.
1.10 — "Vice Versa" (Radio Serial).
1.40 — Interlude.
1.45 — Harold Rhodes (Organ).
2.15 — Three-Band Session.
3.0 — Evensong From Norwich Cathedral.
3.30 — B.B.C. Scottish Orchestra.
4.15 — Merry-Go-Round (Naval Edition).
5.15 — Children's Hour.
6.0 — News. Weather Forecast.
6.30 — Transatlantic Call (The Comic In Our Life).
7.0 — Henry Wood Promenade Concerts.
7.50 — Geraldo And His Orchestra.

8.15 — Brain And Mind (By L. J. Witts).
8.30 — The Will Hay Programme.
9.0 — Big Ben Minute For Reflection. News.
9.15 — Tuesday Serenade.
10.10 — What Can We Learn From The War?
10.25 — Julius Isserlis (Piano).
11.0 — News Summary.
11.3 — Carl Barriteau And His Orchestra.
11.30 — Jack Payne And His Orchestra.
12.0 — Big Ben.

Regional Stations may introduce special items during the evening programme from their own studio or other stations.

LIGHT 1,500 - 261

9.0 a.m. — News.
9.15 — Leslie "Jiver" Hutchinson And His Coloured Orch.
9.45 — Keyboard Cavalcade.
10.0 — Record Album.
11.0 — Rudy Lewis At The Organ.
11.30 — Great Music (Records).
12.15 p.m. — Melodious Moods.
12.30 — News. Interlude.
12.45 — Cricket. (Yorks v. Lancs.)
1.0 — The One O'Clock Story.
1.15 — Repeat Of Sunday Rhapsody.
2.15 — B.B.C. Northern Orchestra.

2.45 — The Robinson Family.
3.0 — Piano Parade (Records).
3.15 — Cricket (Yorks. v. Lancs).
3.30 — Music While You Work.
4.0 — Jazz (Records).
4.15 — I'll Play To You.
4.45 — Harry Fryer And His Orchestra.
5.30 — Flotsam's Follies.
6.0 — Michaeloft And His Mazurka Orchestra.
6.30 — Swing Club (Records).
7.0 — News.
7.10 — Cricket (Yorks. v. Lancs.).
7.15 — Foolish Things.
7.45 — Heifetz (Violin).
8.0 — Carroll Levis Show.
8.45 — Three's Company.
9.0 — Band Of The Life Guards.
9.30 — "I Don't Believe It" (Fantastic Comedy).
10.0 — News.

10.10 — "The Armchair Detective."
10.30 — Debroy Somers And His Band.
11.0 — Golden Slumbers.
11.30 — Felton Rapley At The Theatre Organ.
11.50 — News.
12.0 — Big Ben.

A General Forces Programme is transmitted on the short wave-lengths throughout 24 hours.

73

An early picture of Johnny Mack Brown, who can be seen at the Temp, Lye, next week.

CLIFTON LYE TEL.198

1946

SUNDAY. MAY 19th. Continuous from 4.0 p.m.
Ray Milland, Betty Field, Patricia Morrison in
ARE HUSBANDS NECESSARY (U)
Edith Fellows, Clarence Kolb in FIVE LITTLE PEPPERS (U)

MONDAY, MAY 20th (3 Days):
Daily from 5.0 p.m. Matinee Monday at 2.30 p.m.

A GAINSBOROUGH PICTURE
James MASON · Margaret LOCKWOOD
PATRICIA ROC
The WICKED LADY
With GRIFFITH JONES AND MICHAEL RENNIE
Eagle-Lion Distribution

Mon. 3.10, 5.40, 8.5   Tues. and Wed. 5.40, 8.5
And FULL SUPPORTING PROGRAMME

THURSDAY, MAY 23rd (3 Days):
Daily from 5.0 p.m. Matinee Thursday at 2.30 p.m.
PHILIP DORN, JEAN SULLIVAN, HELMUT DANTINE in
ESCAPE IN THE DESERT (A)

Thurs. 3.30, 6.5, 8.45   Fri. and Sat. 6.5, 8.45
Leon Errol, Elizabeth Risdon, Edwin Maxwell in
MAMA LOVES PAPA (A)
Thurs. at 2.30, 5.5, 7.35   Fri. and Sat. 5.0, 7.30

CHILDREN'S MATINEE EVERY SATURDAY at 1.45 p.m.
Special Programme with Serial, Cartoons and Comedies

52

TEMP LYE

SUN., MAY 19th, 4.0 to 9.30
Warren Hull, Mary Ainslee in
THE SPIDER RETURNS (A)
Also Penny Singleton in
FOOTLIGHT GLAMOUR (U)

MON., MAY 20th (3 Days):
GALE STORM
JOHNNY MACK BROWN
C. A. SMITH in
THE RIGHT TO LIVE (A)

Jean Parker, Tim Ryan in
ADVENTURES OF KITTY
O'DAY

THURS., MAY 23rd (3 Days):
ED GARDNER
VICTOR MOORE
BARRY SULLIVAN
A Parade of Paramount Stars in
DUFFY'S TAVERN (U)
Full Supporting Programme

Matinees Mon. & Thurs. at 2.15
Special Children's Matinee
Sat. 2.15   55

MAJESTIC

CRADLEY HEATH   Tel. 6150
SUPERVISED CAR PARK

MON., MAY 20th (3 Days):
GINGER ROGERS
LANA TURNER in
Week-end at the Waldorf
At 2.45   5.20   8.0   (A)
Full Supporting Programme

THURS., MAY 23rd (3 Days):
FRANCHOT TONE
SUSANNA FOSTER in
That Night With You (A)
At 2.45   5.35   8.35
Basil Rathbone, Nigel Bruce in
PURSUIT TO ALGIERS (U)
At 4.15 and 7.15
Full Supporting Programme

Monday to Friday from 2.15
Saturday at 2.0, 5.20, 8.10
W. SYKES, A.R.C.O., at the
Christie Organ   51

THE ROYAL

CRADLEY HEATH
'Phone 5581
Mats. Mon. and Thurs. at 2.30
Sat. at 2.15

MON., MAY 20th (3 Days):
RAY MILLAND and
JANE WYMAN in
THE LOST WEEK-END
BONNIE LASSIE
PARAMOUNT NEWS

THURS., MAY 23rd (3 Days):
FRED MacMURRAY
JOAN LESLIE and
JUNE HAVER in
WHERE DO WE GO
FROM HERE?
Technicolor
ALWAYS GOODBYE
PARAMOUNT NEWS   57

THE GRAND

OLD HILL
phone 6161 CRADLEY

MON., MAY 20th (3 Days):
FRANK SINATRA
JACK HALEY
MICHELE MORGAN in
HIGHER AND HIGHER
Full Supporting Programme
Comedies, Etc.

No. 7: JUNGLE QUEEN

THURS., MAY 23rd (3 Days):
WALTER HUSTON
RUTH CHATTERTON in
DODSWORTH
Full Supporting Programme
UNIVERSAL NEWS   56

REX

TEL. 1608
CAR PARK
BLACKHEATH

MON., MAY 20th (3 Days):
RICHARD ARLEN
CHERYL WALKER in
IDENTITY UNKNOWN
Judy Canova, Allan Jones in
TRUE TO THE ARMY

THURS., MAY 23rd (3 Days):
CAROL RAYE, ANN ZEIGLER
WEBSTER BOOTH in
WALTZ TIME
Martha Driscoll in
UNDER WESTERN SKIES   50

Frank Sinatra appears at the Grand Cinema, Old Hill, 20th May 1946.

Lilliput Marionette Theatre in operation, Netherton
Library & Arts Centre, October 1947.

Pepita Sarazena and Juan Granero in "Spanish Rhapsody",
Wulfrun Hall, Wolverhampton, 11th November 1947.

"Gaslight", Sedgley Players, December 1951.

24.9.51

GRAND THEATRE, W'HAMPTON.
Telephone 22675.
Monday to Friday at 7.15. Saturday at 5.30 and 8.0. Matinee Wednesday at 2.30.
Derek Salberg and Basil Thomas's Wolverhampton Repertory Company in
MURDER AT THE VICARAGE.
Adapted by Moie Charles and Barbara Toy from the novel by Agatha Christie. For TWO WEEKS, commencing Oct. 1:
MILD AND BITTER.
The Repertory Revue for 1951.

DUDLEY HIPPODROME.—Nightly at 7.30. Sat. 5.0 & 8.0. Mat. Thurs. at 2.30. NATIONAL LIGHT OPERA CO. in CHU CHIN CHOW (Mon to Wed.). Sun., Sept. 30, at 7.30: Humphrey Lyttleton & his Band. Neva Raphaello. Bkg. 10-9

PLAZA THEATRE, WEST BROMWICH.—At 6.30 and 8.30. STRIKE A NUDE NOTE. Cyril Dowler, Rhoda Rogers, Sam Linfield and Co., Bill Hancox. Oct. 1: BON SOIR, MESDAMES. Box office 10-9. Wes 0030, or Lewis's.

BIRMINGHAM HIPPODROME.—At 6.15 & 8.30. The All-Male Comedy Show, SOLDIERS IN SKIRTS. Joe Stein, Louis Hayden, Dumarte & Denzen, Tib-Boult, Reggie Redcliffe. Oct. 1: ARTHUR ENGLISH. Box office 10-8, or Beatties.

THEATRE ROYAL, BIRMINGHAM. Evgs. at 7.0. Mats. Thurs. & Sat., 2.30. OKLAHOMA. Music by Richard Rodgers. Book & lyrics by Oscar Hammerstein II. Oct. 8 (2 weeks): Annie Get Your Gun. Box office 10-8, or Beatties.

GAUMONT, WOLVERHAMPTON.—Doors open at 1.40. Richard Greene & Barbara Hale in LORNA DOONE (U). Tech. At 3.15, 6.10 and 9.0. Also, Wayne Morris in THE BIG GUSHER (U). At 1.50, 4.40 and 7.35.

QUEEN'S, WOLVERHAMPTON.—Basil Radford, Jimmy Hanley and Janette Scott in THE GALLOPING MAJOR (U). At 3.27, 6.15 and 9.0. Elsie Randolph & Jack MacNaughton in CHEER THE BRAVE (U). 2.1, 4.49, 7.37.

ODEON, WOLVERHAMPTON.—James Stewart, Marlene Dietrich, Jack Hawkins & Glynis Johns in NO HIGHWAY (U). At 2.0, 5.25, 8.45. Dorothy Patrick, DESTINATION BIG HOUSE (A). At 4.0 & 7.25. Last complete perf., 7.0.

SAVOY (A.B.C.), W'TON 22917.—Doors open at 12.30. Continuous from 12.45. Moira Shearer, Robert Helpmann & Leonide Massine in TALES OF HOFFMAN (A). Tech. At 12.45, 3.15, 5.50, 8.35. Look to the Forest (U) 2.35, 5.10, 7.50.

CLIFTON, WOLVERHAMPTON.—David Brian & Suzanne Dalbert in BREAKTHROUGH (A). At 2.36, 5.43 & 8.50. Leon Errol & Joe Kirkwood, jun., HUMPHREY TAKES A CHANCE (U). At 1.26, 4.22, 7.29. Last complete prog. 7.18.

COLISEUM, WOLVERHAMPTON.—Lucille Ball in THE AFFAIRS OF SALLY (U). Jon Hall in ON THE ISLE OF SAMOA (U). King of the Rocketmen, Episode 8.

OLYMPIA, WOLVERHAMPTON.—Lucille Ball in THE AFFAIRS OF SALLY (U). Jon Hall in ON THE ISLE OF SAMOA (U). King of the Rocketmen, Episode 8.

PENN CINEMA.—Barbara Stanwyck and Walter Huston in THE FURIES (A). At 2.10, 5.35 and 9.0. John Lund in MY FRIEND IRMA (U). At 3.45 and 9.10. Thurs.: Gary Cooper, NORTH-WEST MOUNTED POLICE (A).

EMPIRE, WALSALL.—James Stewart and Marlene Dietrich in NO HIGHWAY (U). At 3.0, 5.20 and 8.40. Also, SQUARE DANCE JUBILEE (U). At 4.0 and 7.20. Universal News. Last programme at 7.20.

PALACE, GREAT BRIDGE.—Evgs. doors open at 5.30. Sundays at 3.30. James Ellison in I KILLED GERONIMO (A). David Bruce in TIMBER FURY (U). Kirk Alyn in Daughter of Don Q. Episode 9.

PICTUREDROME, DARLASTON.—David Farrar, Nadia Gray & June Clyde, NIGHT WITHOUT STARS (A). Atom Man v. Superman, Ep. 4. Turpin v. Robinson Return Fight. Thursday: BEDTIME FOR BONZO (U).

REGAL CINEMA, DARLASTON.—Sidney Tafler and Katherine Blake, ASSASSIN FOR HIRE (A).
Arthur Lucan and Kitty McShane in OLD MOTHER RILEY AT HOME (A).
Turpin v. Robinson Return Fight.

SAVOY (A.B.C.), WALSALL 2444.—Moira Shearer, Robert Helpmann & Leonide Massine in
TALES OF HOFFMAN (U).
At 2.35, 4.35, 6.50 and 9.5.
Plus the world's best newsreel—Pathe.

AVION, Aldridge.—Googie Withers and Petula Clark in WHITE CORRIDORS (U). At 5.40 and 8.38.
CARLTON.—Adv. Bkg. Tel. 21594. John Garfield, BREAKING POINT (A). THE LADY TAKES A SAILOR.
CLIFTON, Coseley.—TREASON (A). At 5.35 and 8.40. Also, THE SECOND MATE (U). At 7.0 only.
CLIFTON, Fallings Park.—Charles Bickford, TREASON (A). 2.21, 5.37, 8.53. THE SECOND MATE (U). 4.6, 7.22.
CLIFTON, Sedgley.—Kirk Douglas in ACE IN THE HOLE (A). 5.5, 8.35. Mona Freeman, DEAR BRAT (U). 7.0.
CLIFTON, Wellington.—Judy Holliday in BORN YESTERDAY (A). Glenn Ford, THE FLYING MISSILE (U).
CRITERION, Dudley.—ONE WILD OAT (A). At 2.10, 5.40 and 9.10. TARGET UNKNOWN (U). 3.55 & 7.25.
DALE, Willenhall.—Gordon McRae in RETURN OF THE FRONTIERSMAN (U). Tech. PRETTY BABY (U).
GAUMONT, Dudley.—LORNA DOONE (U). Tech. At 3.0, 6.0, 9.0. THE BIG GUSHER (U). 1.30, 4.30, 7.30.
GAUMONT, Wednesbury.—ACE IN THE HOLE (A). At 2.55, 5.10 & 8.46. Also, DEAR BRAT (U). At 1.15 and 7.5.
IMPERIAL (A.B.C.), Walsall 2565.—Greer Garson, Gregory Peck, VALLEY OF DECISION (A). THE INLANDERS.
ODEON, Bilston.—Stewart Granger, Walter Pidgeon, SOLDIERS THREE (U). Also, HOME TOWN STORY (A).
ODEON, Bloxwich.—Dana Andrews in A WALK IN THE SUN (A). Robert Paige in FRONTIER BADMAN.
ODEON, Dudley.—James Stewart, NO HIGHWAY (U). 2.0, 5.25, 8.50. DESTINATION BIG HOUSE (A). 4.0, 7.25.
ODEON, Dunstall.—Today, WHITE CORRIDORS (A). 2.20, 5.30 & 8.40. MY TRUE STORY (A). At 4.0 & 7.10.
ODEON, Stafford.—James Stewart, NO HIGHWAY (U). At 2.0, 5.25 & 8.40. DESTINATION BIG HOUSE (A).
OLYMPIA (A.B.C.), Darlaston, 19.
John Wayne in
RIO GRANDE (U).
PICTURE HOUSE, Sedgley.—John Garfield in THE BREAKING POINT (A). Dead End Kids on Dress Parade.
PICTURE HOUSE, Willenhall.—ANNIE GET YOUR GUN (U). 3.15, 5.45, 8.35. SAMOA (U). 2.30, 5.0, 7.46.
PLAZA, Dudley.—Today: STORM WARNING (A). At 3.15, 5.55, 8.36. THE FAR FRONTIER (U). 2.5, 4.45, 7.25.
REGAL, Wednesfield.—WHITE CORRIDORS (A). At 5.35 and 8.45. MY TRUE STORY (A). At 7.20 only.
REGENT, Tipton.—Ray Milland in COPPER CANYON (U). Technicolor. Also, KING OF ALCATRAZ (A).
REX, Whitmore Reans.—Marjorie Main in PA AND MA KETTLE (U). Also, BUTCH MINDS THE BABY (A).
ROSUM, Leamore.—TARGET UN-

HIPPODROME, W'HAMPTON.—
6.15. Telephone 21626l. 8.30.
THE SPICE OF PARIS.
A Gay and Funny Revue.
Big Cast of International Favourites.
Carnival Tuesday, both performances.
Prizes and Surprises.
Next Week: The Famous Royal Command Star, Johnny Lockwood in
KRAZY KNIGHTS.

THEATRE ROYAL, BILSTON.—
Telephone 41001.
Monday to Friday at 7.30. Saturday at 6.0 and 8.0.
D. S. Productions present,
AWAY FROM THEM ALL.
With BALLIOL and MERTON (world's most sensational act). Thrills! Thrills! 3 Bennett Brothers (music hath charm). Bob Nelson (Ain't plums cheap?). Bert Brook, Vic Leonard, Gabriele, The Royadtys, the Welcome Singers (from the B.B.C.'s Welsh Rarebit). A real treat.

DAVID GARRICK, LICHFIELD.—Evenings at 7.15. Saturdays also at 4.30. RANDOM HARVEST. An adaptation of James Hilton's famous love story. October 1: SIT DOWN A MINUTE, ADRIAN. Box office 10.30—8. Tel. 3112.

SHREWSBURY REPERTORY THEATRE.—Tel. 2144. Monday to Friday 7.15. Saturday at 6.15 and 8.30. This Week: The Beacon Players present MASTER OF ARTS, by William Douglas Home. Oct 1: COUNT YOUR BLESSINGS.

Concerts, Dances, &c.

WOLVERHAMPTON AMATEUR DRAMA REPERTORY SEASON
GOODYEAR AMATEUR DRAMATIC SOCIETY (in association with the Cultural and Entertainments Committee)
present
LITTLE LAMBS EAT IVY
A Comedy by Noel Langley
At the WULFRUN HALL THEATRE
On THURSDAY and FRIDAY NEXT, SEPTEMBER 27 and 28, at 7.30 p.m.
RESERVED TICKETS 3/6 and 2/6.
UNRESERVED 1/6
Obtainable at the Civic Hall Booking Office

WOLVERHAMPTON FILM SOCIETY
(In association with the Cultural and Entertainments Committee)
WULFRUN HALL
TOMORROW (TUES.), SEPTEMBER 25, 7.30.
Emil Jannings in THE BROKEN JUG (Germany, 1937)
With AVALANCHE PATROL
MEMBERS ONLY REFRESHMENTS
DISCUSSION
All Inquiries for Membership to: Hon. Secretary, Civic Hall. Telephone 21359

FESTIVAL OF BRITAIN,
1851—1951

HENRY MEADOWS LTD. EMPLOYEES WELFARE FUND
GALA DANCE
FRIDAY, OCTOBER 5, 1951
CIVIC HALL
Dancing 8 p.m. to 12 midnight to REG BARTLAM WITH HIS BROADCASTING BAND
TICKETS 3/-
NO ADMITTANCE AFTER 10 p.m. WITH OR WITHOUT A TICKET
Licensed Refreshments

CIVIC HALL,
WOLVERHAMPTON
TONIGHT (MON.), SEPTEMBER 24,
7.30 till 11.30 p.m.
RONNIE HANCOX AND HIS BAND
TICKETS 3/- (at door)
SATURDAY NEXT, SEPT. 29, 1951
7.30 till 11.30 p.m.
REG BARTLAM AND HIS BROADCASTING ORCHESTRA
TICKETS 3/- (in advance)
NO ADMISSION AFTER 10 p.m.

THE GEORGE THOMAS QUINTET
Runners-up in the All Britain Dance Band Championship 1950; Wiltshire Champions 1950; Staffordshire Champions 1950; Heart of England Champions 1950; Nottinghamshire Champions 1951; Heart of the Midlands Champions 1951; Mid-Britain Area Champions 1951. May we quote you for your next event? George Thomas, 27, Paget St., Wolverhampton.
Telephone 23231

E. P. JENKS (Mixed) YOUTH CLUB, Bilston Road, GRAND SOCIAL. Free, Tomorrow (Tues.), Sept. 25, to which old and new members are cordially invited. Guests of the evening: Beckminster Questors
Start 8 p.m. Open to Employees and Non-Employees, 14 to 21 years.

A WARM welcome is extended to old and new friends at the
UPPER GORNAL SOCIAL AND SPORTS CLUB, CLARENCE STREET
WHIST DRIVES
EVERY TUESDAY at 7.30 p.m.
TICKETS, Price 1/3, at the Door.
Drives recommence TOMORROW (TUESDAY), SEPTEMBER 25.

PALAIS DE DANSE, Temple Street, WOLVERHAMPTON
Tuesdays, Thursdays, Fridays
7.30 till 10.30 p.m. Admission 2/-
Saturdays at 7 p.m. Admission 2/6
Write or Call for Private Lessons

ST. PAUL'S HALL. Dancing Tonight, also every Thursday 7.30 till 10.30 JACK ANDREWS'S BAND. Admission 1/-. Grand Dance every Saturday 7.30 till 11 p.m. Jack Andrews and His Band. Admission 2/-. Maple Floor. Ices. Buffet.

ST. TERESA'S, PARKFIELDS,
OLD-TIME DANCE EVERY TUESDAY, 7.45-10.45 p.m.
Music by H. JONES, JUN. M.C. Mr. P. Barnett, A.E.S.T.D., O.T.B. Adm. 1/6.
Whist Drive every Thurs., 7.30. Adm. 1/3

ST. Teresa's, Parkfield. Old-Time Carnival Dance, Tomorrow (Tuesday), September 25, 7.45-11 p.m. H. JONES JUN. ORCHESTRA. M.C.: Mr. P. Barnett, A.E.S.T.D., O.T.B. ADMISSION 2/-

CONSERVATIVE HALL, Dudley Port, Tipton. Old-Tyme Dance. Re-opening Tomorrow, Tuesday, September 25, 8 p.m. to 10.30 p.m. Adm. 1/6. Old and new patrons welcomed. M.C.: Mr. D. Edwards.

DON'T Forget, Thurs. Next (7.30-11). Conservative Club, Whitmore Reans. Carnival Old-Time Dance. Introducing the Crystall Tango. Adm. 2/-.

OLD-TIME DANCE, Crown Hotel, Codsall, Tuesday, 8 till 11. M.C.: A. Gardner.

LEARN TO DANCE NOW! Absolute Beginners Class every Wednesday, 8-10.30 p.m. 1/6. Donaghy Dance Studio, New Street, Dudley.

OLD-TIME CLASS, Holy Rosary, Hickman Avenue, off Willenhall Rd. Every Tuesday at 8. Admission 1/3.

THE Fieldhouse, Codsall Road. Modern Dancing Tonight and every Mon. 8-11. Adm. 2/-. The Premier Dance Band.

PARTNER WHIST DRIVE, Tomorrow, Tuesday, Penn Secondary Schl. Manor Rd. Commence 7.30. Adm. 1/6. All welcome.

James Stewart appears in "No Highway" at the Odeon Cinemas at Wolverhampton, Dudley and Stafford and at the Empire, Walsall, this week.

Gilbert Harding, whose TV appearances in the panel game "What's My Line" drew audiences of 11 million in the 1950's, attended Wolverhampton's Royal Orphanage as a pupil in 1916. The school is now The Royal Wolverhampton School.

Gwen Berryman

Invites you to see her stock of Summer Dresses, Blouses and Dress Skirts, at reasonable prices.

Larger sizes in good styles, always in stock, also Underwear and Baby-wear.

"RITA" 1.5.50

24, Worcester Street, Wolverhampton.

David Farrar in "Night Without Stars" at the Picturedome, Darlaston.

15.2.52

CLARKSON ROSE, the Dudley born actor-producer-manager, and "Twinkle," his intimate musical, will be going on the road once more on March 17.

This will be the 32nd consecutive touring season of the show, which began very modestly as a six-handed pierrot troupe on Ryde Pier on Whit Saturday, 1921, its takings being £16. To-day "Twinkle" can "play the best seaside dates" and some of the principal inland theatres. Its personnel of six is nowadays more like 20, and its modest presentation has grown into an elaborate production with many changes of scene and set. Yet basically it remains what it was at the beginning—a jolly inconsequential succession of song, dance, comedy, of "singles" and "concerteds," with the element of personal popularity emphasised all the time.

Gwen Berryman, "Doris Archer" in the BBC's radio serial "The Archers" and one of Wolverhampton's famous daughters.

The Malcolm Mitchell Trio. Malcolm (centre) can be seen, with his full orchestra, at the Windsor, Bearwood, this Sunday, 18th September 1955.

DELANEY BREAKS DUDLEY RECORD

The Eric Delaney Band broke the house record at Dudley Hippodrome last Sunday—only a week after it had been established by Sid Phillips. On the strength of this success, the Delaney Band has been booked to give two more performances in January.

Geraldo has been added to the list of future Sunday attractions, and will play his first concert at the theatre on December 12.

Other dates include: Lou Preager (October 31), Harry Gold (November 7), Ronnie Scott (14th), Vic Lewis (21st), Johnny Dankworth (28th) and the Squadronaires (December 5). *1954*

Beryl Reid, seen here in one of her other character guises, as the naughty schoolgirl "Monica", appears at the Dudley Hippodrome for the season, 1955.

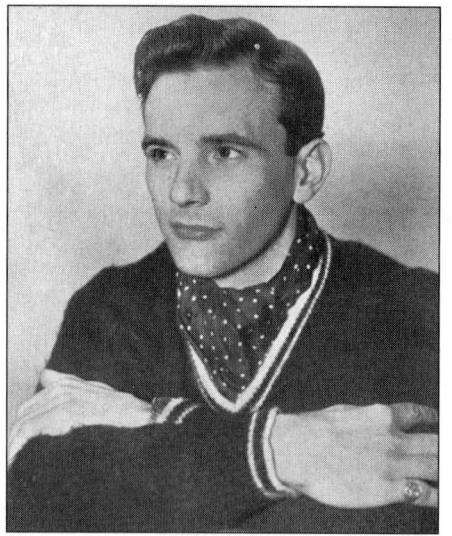

Dennis Lotis tops the bill at the Windsor Theatre, week commencing 24th October 1955.

THE WINDSOR THEATRE

Tel: BEA 2244 BEARWOOD Tel: BEA 2244

Proprietors: HEWITSONS LTD.

Managing Director ... ... GEOFFREY HEWITSON
House Manager and Licensee ... ... JOHN E. KING
Windsor Orchestra under the Direction of LAURI LAMBERT
Stage Manager } W. E. SCRIVENS
Electrician } For Hewitsons Ltd. ... S. T. JONES
Publicity } ... LAWSON TROUT PUBLICITY LTD.

PRICES OF ADMISSION
(including Tax)

	Twice Nightly	Sundays
ORCHESTRA STALLS	3/6	Seats at
CENTRE STALLS	2/6	
SIDE STALLS	2/6	
PIT STALLS	1/6	5/-
FRONT CIRCLE	3/6	4/-
REAR CIRCLE	2/3	3/-
UNRESERVED SEATS	1/-	

Reduced Prices for all Matinees

Monday and Tuesday First House Old Age Pensioners 1/-

FOR PARTY CONCESSION APPLY TO MANAGER

Advance Booking Office open daily (except Sun.) 10-0—8-0

Telephone Bookings accepted for all Performances

PRIVATE (free) CAR PARK :: LICENSED LOUNGE

WEEK COMMENCING MONDAY, OCTOBER 24th, 1955.

1. OVERTURE
2. EL VANTIS .... Roping them in
3. DON ELLIS .... The Commissionaire
4. McKAY SISTERS .... Two Smart Girls
5. TOMMY LOCKY .... The Unusual Entertainer
6. THE FLYING VOLEROS .... Britain's Premier Aerial Presentation

INTERVAL

7. McKAY SISTERS .... A wee drop o' Scotch
8. THE TWO NADIAS .... Continental Jugglers
9. CARVEY & MAC .... Foolish Moments
10. The Dynamic Song Stylist
DENNIS LOTIS
Films, Television and Recording Star.
NORMAN MURRELLS at the Piano.

THE QUEEN

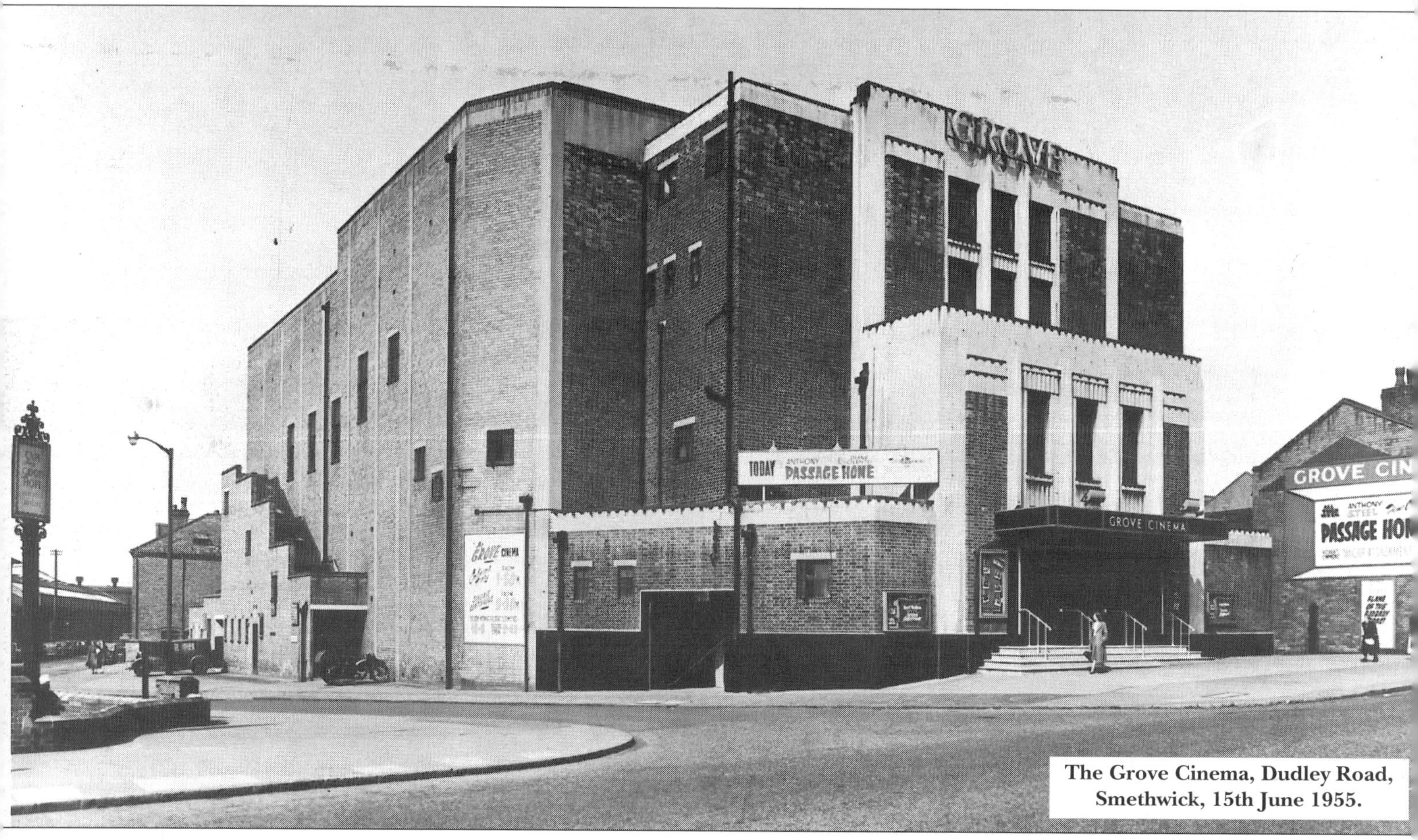

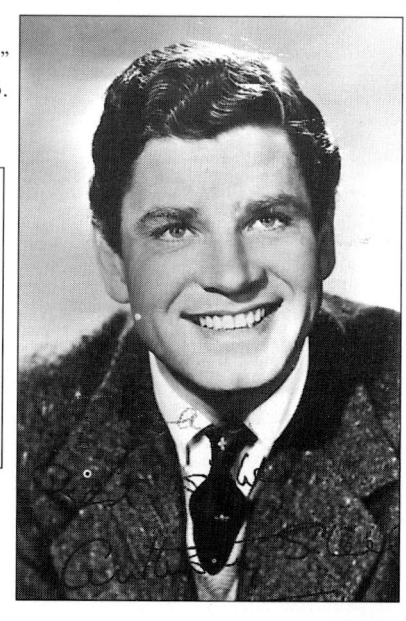

The Grove Cinema, Dudley Road, Smethwick, 15th June 1955.

It's a white Christmas

BECAUSE, of petrol rationing it was stay-at-home Christmas holiday in the Midlands.

Just as well. It was a White Christmas — the first for 18 years.

On a brighter note, comedians Morecambe and Wise were second top-of-the-bill in "Dick Whittington" at the Dudley Hippodrome. A critic of the day described them as "a constant laugh." 1956

Anthony Steel appears in "Passage Home" at the Grove Cinema this week, June 1955.

A MUSICAL EVENING

On Saturday 9th December a Musical Evening was held at the Salvation Army Hall, Stirchley when members of the Warley Songsters and the Warley Band gave a very enjoyable programme.

Lt. W. Dinsmore opened the meeting with the hymn "Climbing up the golden stairs", and S/Co. Leader C. Bartram led the prayers after which the Songsters sang "Follow thou Me".

After the introduction of the Chairman, the recitation "Unawares" was given by C/Sec. Mrs. Kirby and Lt. Leggett sang "The Star in the East" followed by Songster Mrs. Foxall who gave a moving testimony of her experience of the love and power of God.

The Band then played "Glad entrance" and other items and the Songsters sang "Pentecostal Fire". Then S/Co. Leader C. Bartram and Y.P.Bd/Ldr. M. Porter played a cornet duet "Hopes Fair Haven". Margaret Parkes gave a vocal solo "I'm in His Hands". Then the Warley Timbrelists, under the direction of Capt. Edwards gave a Timbrel Item accompanied by the Band, and two members of the band C. S. M. Foxall and Bro. J. Kirby gave a concertina and violin duet.

This was followed by Capt. Edwards with a monologue "Love is Kind" and after the reading by Mrs. Durrell of Psalm 96 the Band played a Selection "Wondrous Jesus". Lt. Dinsmore thanked all who had taken part and the evening closed with the singing of a Benediction.

1961

"Oklahoma!", Bilston Operatic Company, 1957. This was the final production at Bilston Theatre Royal before demolition.

Members of the Good Companions' Club take part in a Nativity Play, Kingswinford Community Centre, December 1957.

The City of Birmingham Symphony Orchestra rehearse at Dudley Town Hall, 1961.

ABC Cinema, Bilston Street/Garrick Street, Wolverhampton, 1961.

THE
KENDALL-BOND OPERATIC COMPANY
(Affiliated to The National Operatic and Dramatic Association)

PRESENTS

THE FAMOUS MUSICAL PLAY
IN TWO ACTS

ANNIE GET YOUR GUN

(by arrangement with Emile Littler and Chappell and Co., Ltd.)
Music and Lyrics by IRVING BERLIN
Book by HERBERT and DOROTHY FIELDS

WINDSOR THEATRE, BEARWOOD

WEEK COMMENCING

Monday, 5th October, 1959, at 7.15 p.m.

•

Production by EDWARD ATTWOOD

Choreography by MADGE JENKS

THE FREDERICK KENDALL ORCHESTRA
under the direction of JACK MYERS

A trainee projectionist, ABC Cinema, Wolverhampton, 1967.

A Concert of Popular Music by
TCHAIKOWSKY, MOZART
and J. STRAUSS

by the

BIRMINGHAM PHILHARMONIC ORCHESTRA
Leader: Leslie Bowren   *Conductor:* KENNETH PAGE

Soloist: RUTH HANSON
(Mozart Piano Concerto K466)
in

THE CIVIC HALL, BRIERLEY HILL

On SUNDAY, 2nd DECEMBER, 1962

at 7.30 p.m.

_____

ADMISSION 3s. 6d.

Tony Hancock (right) exchanges a joke with his brother,
Roger, 1963.

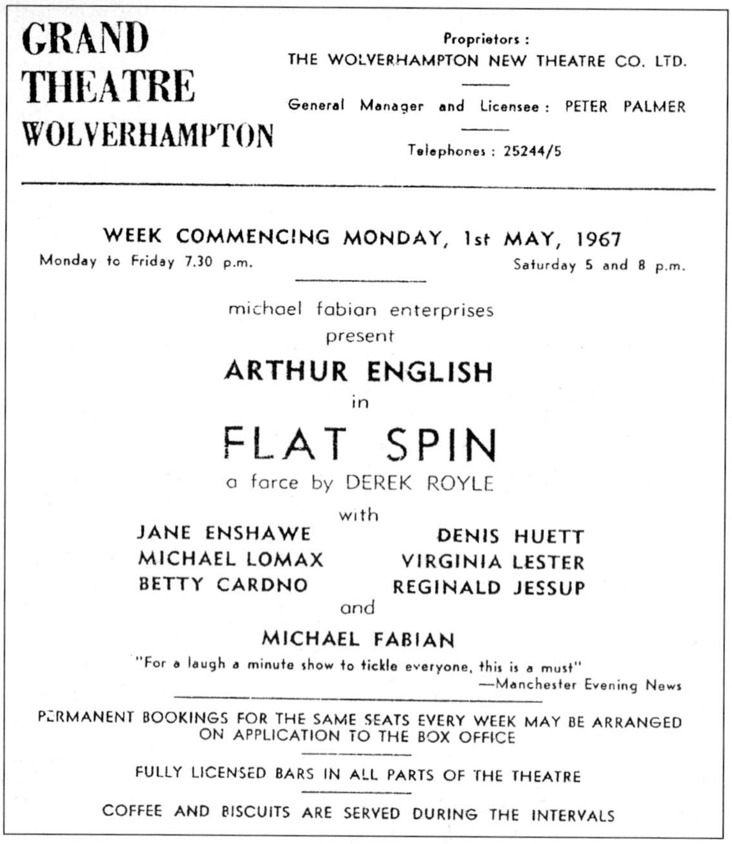

GRAND THEATRE WOLVERHAMPTON

Proprietors :
THE WOLVERHAMPTON NEW THEATRE CO. LTD.

General Manager and Licensee : PETER PALMER

Telephones : 25244/5

WEEK COMMENCING MONDAY, 1st MAY, 1967

Monday to Friday 7.30 p.m.   Saturday 5 and 8 p.m.

michael fabian enterprises
present

ARTHUR ENGLISH

in

FLAT SPIN

a farce by DEREK ROYLE

with

JANE ENSHAWE   DENIS HUETT
MICHAEL LOMAX   VIRGINIA LESTER
BETTY CARDNO   REGINALD JESSUP

and

MICHAEL FABIAN

"For a laugh a minute show to tickle everyone, this is a must"
—Manchester Evening News

PERMANENT BOOKINGS FOR THE SAME SEATS EVERY WEEK MAY BE ARRANGED
ON APPLICATION TO THE BOX OFFICE

FULLY LICENSED BARS IN ALL PARTS OF THE THEATRE

COFFEE AND BISCUITS ARE SERVED DURING THE INTERVALS

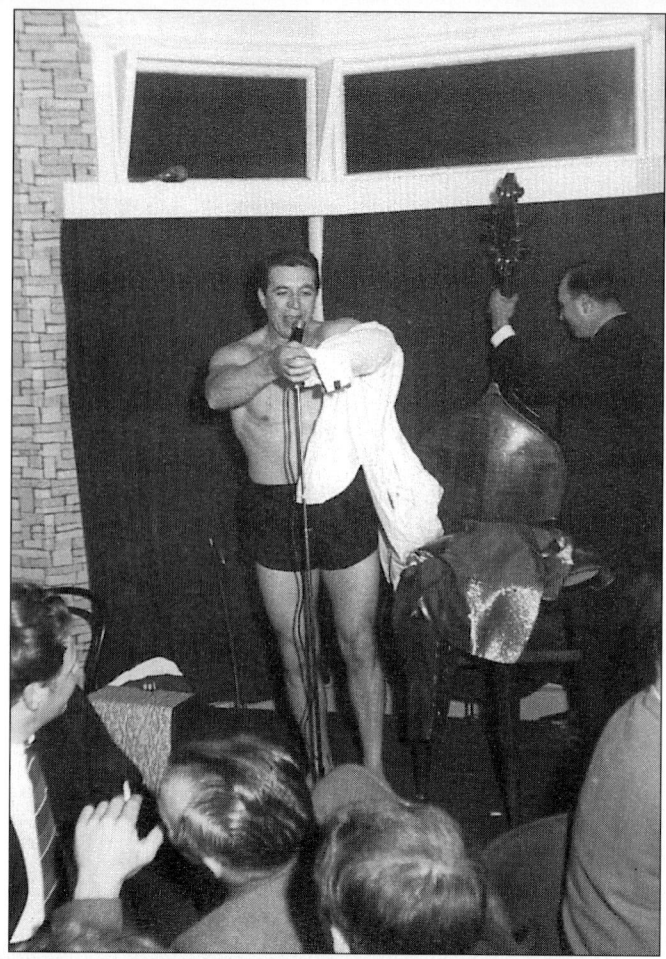

Smethwick comedian, Andy "Muscles running to fat" Wade, 1968. These days Andy has a different career as one of the area's foremost children's entertainers.

Clarkson Rose, one of the most famous of all Pantomime Dames, with some of the juvenile dancers of the Latour Troupe, on his return to his home town of Dudley, December 1964.

Kings Cinema, West Bromwich, 1968.

NOW

A RIOT ON
THE BIG SCREEN

IN COLOR

WARREN MITCHELL
AS ALF GARNETT
TILL DEATH US DO PART

THE LONDON
NOBODY KNOWS

VISIT THE STARLITE BAR
OPEN WEEKDAYS 6 00
SUNDAY 7 00

KINGS

KINGS
Licensed Bar

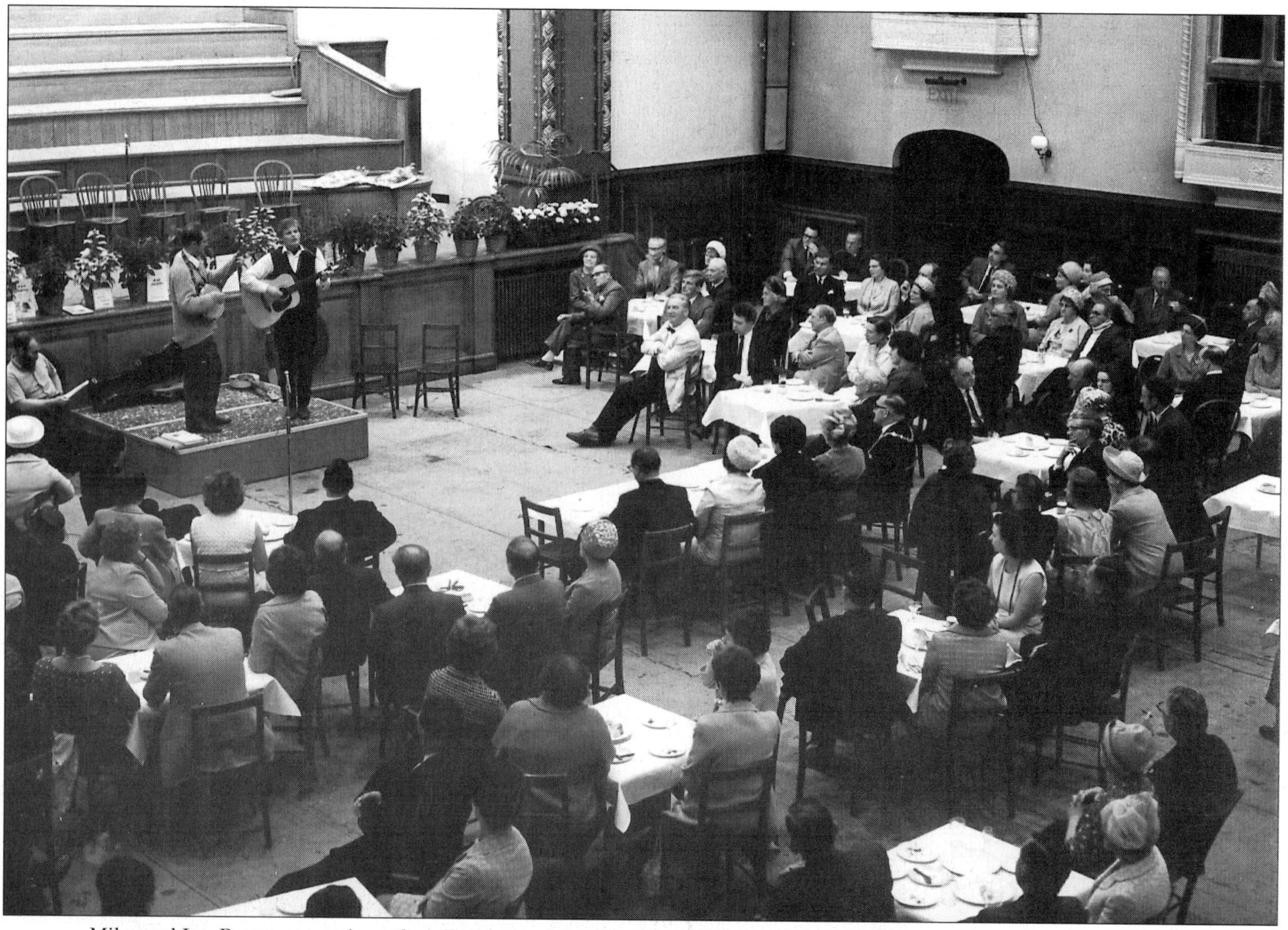

Mike and Jon Raven entertain at the official opening of the Black Country Exhibition, Dudley Town Hall, August 1967.

Dudley Youth Theatre, c. 1970.

TRUCKERS PARADISE
COUNTRY MUSIC CLUB

Grand
C & W Jubilee Dance

AT THE HEN & CHICKENS,
Wolverhampton Road, Warley.
ON MONDAY, JUNE 6th. 8 - 12
featuring
Iron Horse
plus 1971

Late Bar Tickets £1 Meals

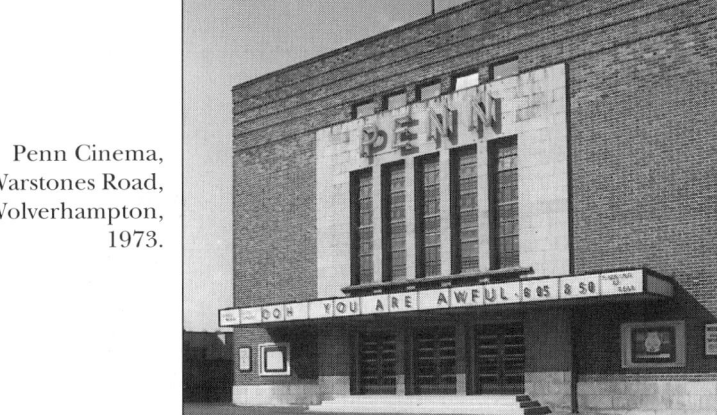

Penn Cinema, Warstones Road, Wolverhampton, 1973.

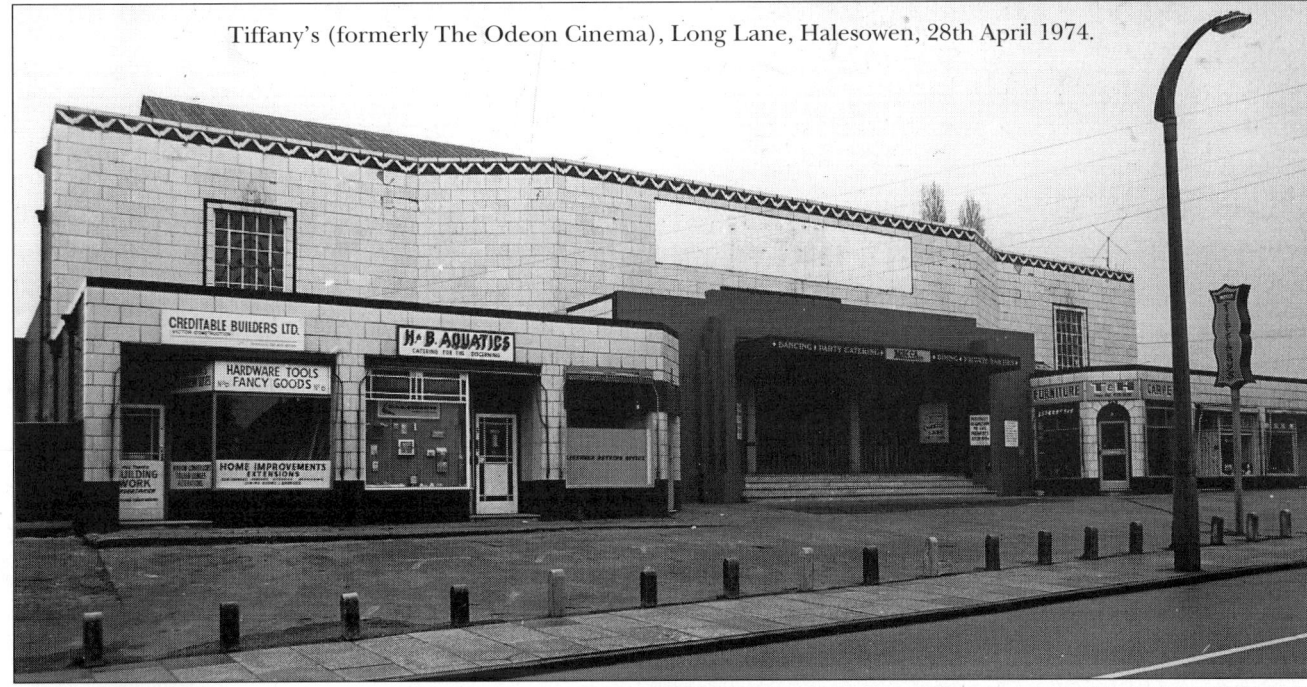

Tiffany's (formerly The Odeon Cinema), Long Lane, Halesowen, 28th April 1974.

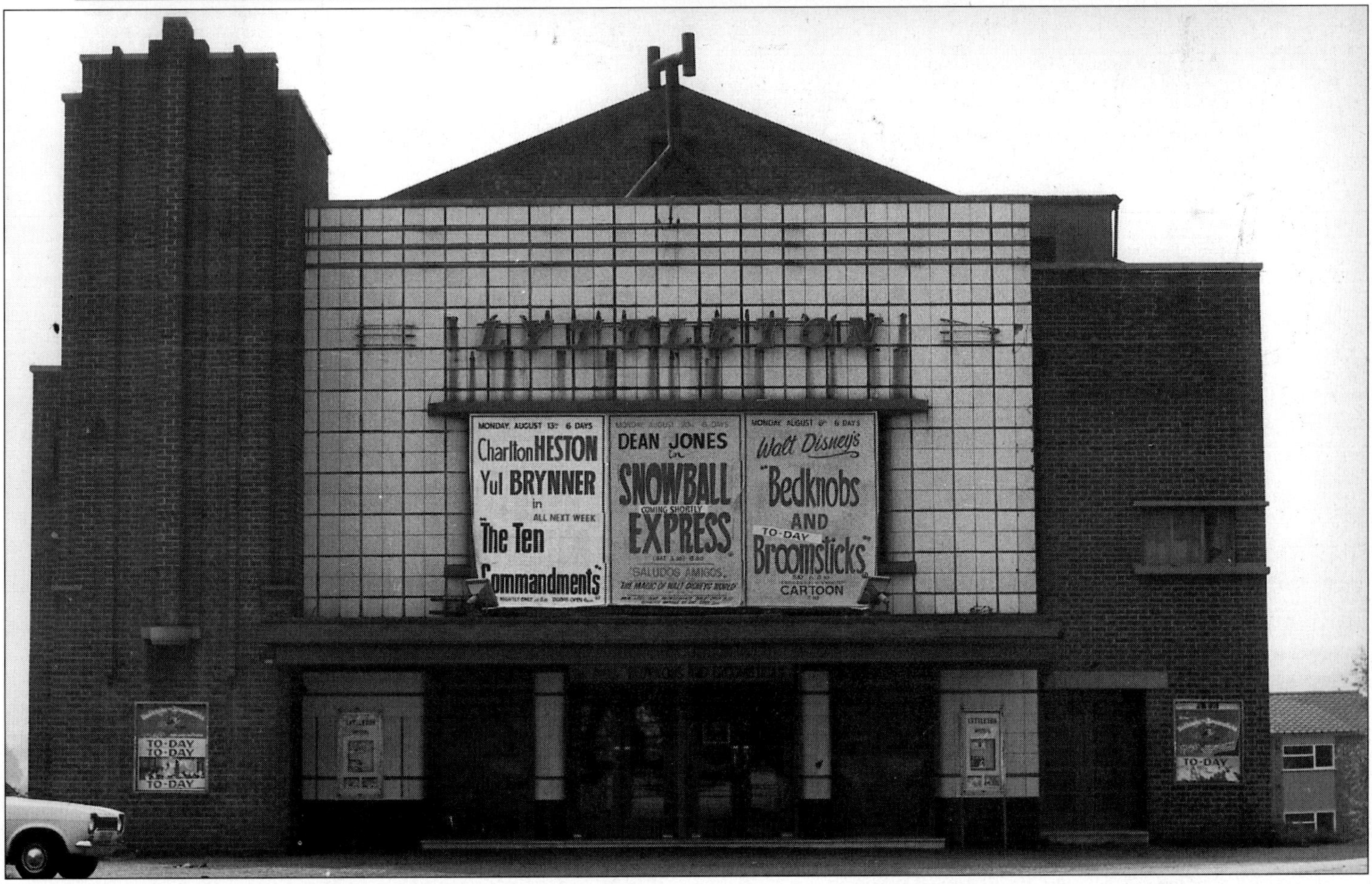

The Lyttleton Cinema, Hagley Road, Halesowen, 12th August 1973.

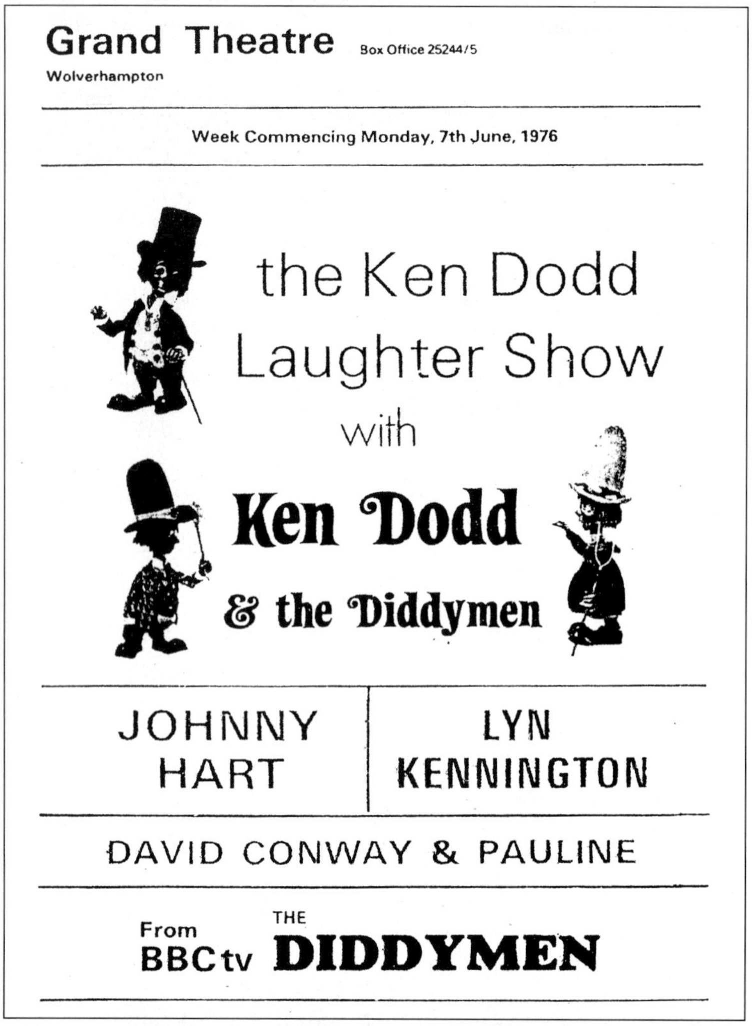

Grand Theatre Box Office 25244/5
Wolverhampton

Week Commencing Monday, 7th June, 1976

the Ken Dodd
Laughter Show
with

 **Ken Dodd**
& the Diddymen

JOHNNY HART	LYN KENNINGTON

DAVID CONWAY & PAULINE

From
BBCtv **THE DIDDYMEN**

David and Pauline Conway ("Music worth watching"), always a popul[ar] act. They were a huge hit on the "Barrymore" TV Show in April 1994.

Jon Raven, Tommy Mundon, Dolly Allen, Harry Harrison and Brian Clift, members of the famous "Black Country Night Out" show, April 1977.

Housewife at the top

JUNE is turning out to be a happy month for Anne Beverley, the singer, whose home is in Netherton, Dudley. She has been booked to appear this month at the most famous variety theatre in the country — the London Palladium. Miss Beverley, who mixes cabaret work with being a housewife and mother, makes her appearance on June 23. And I gather that another Midlander will be on the same bill: Alton Douglas, the King's Norton, Birmingham, comedian. A nice coincidence, because it's the first time at the Palladium for both artists. 1974

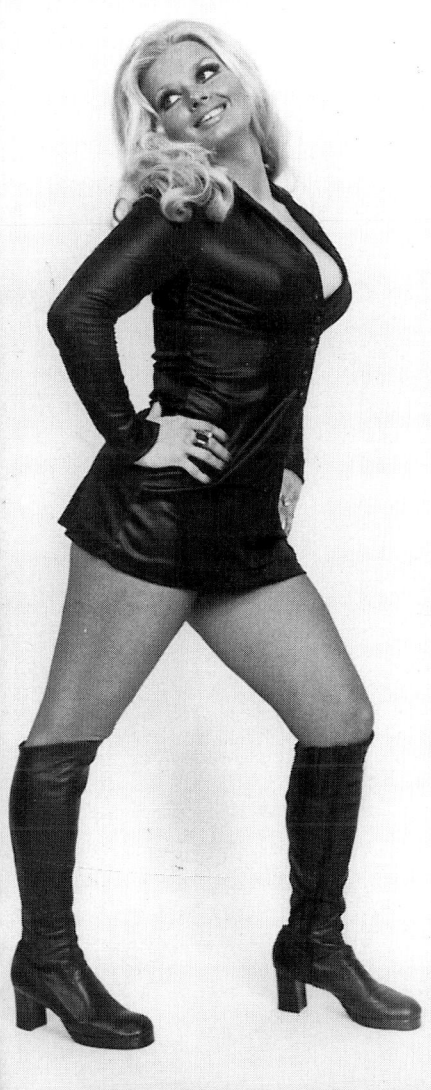

Anne Beverley.

COME TO CANADA

with the original

" OFF THE CUFF "

BLACK COUNTRY NIGHT OUT SHOW 1979

Sue Ashley, Sandra Bird and Elaine Billingham, limber-up for Oldbury Repertory Players' production of "Extravaganza" at The Barlow Theatre Centre, July 1979.

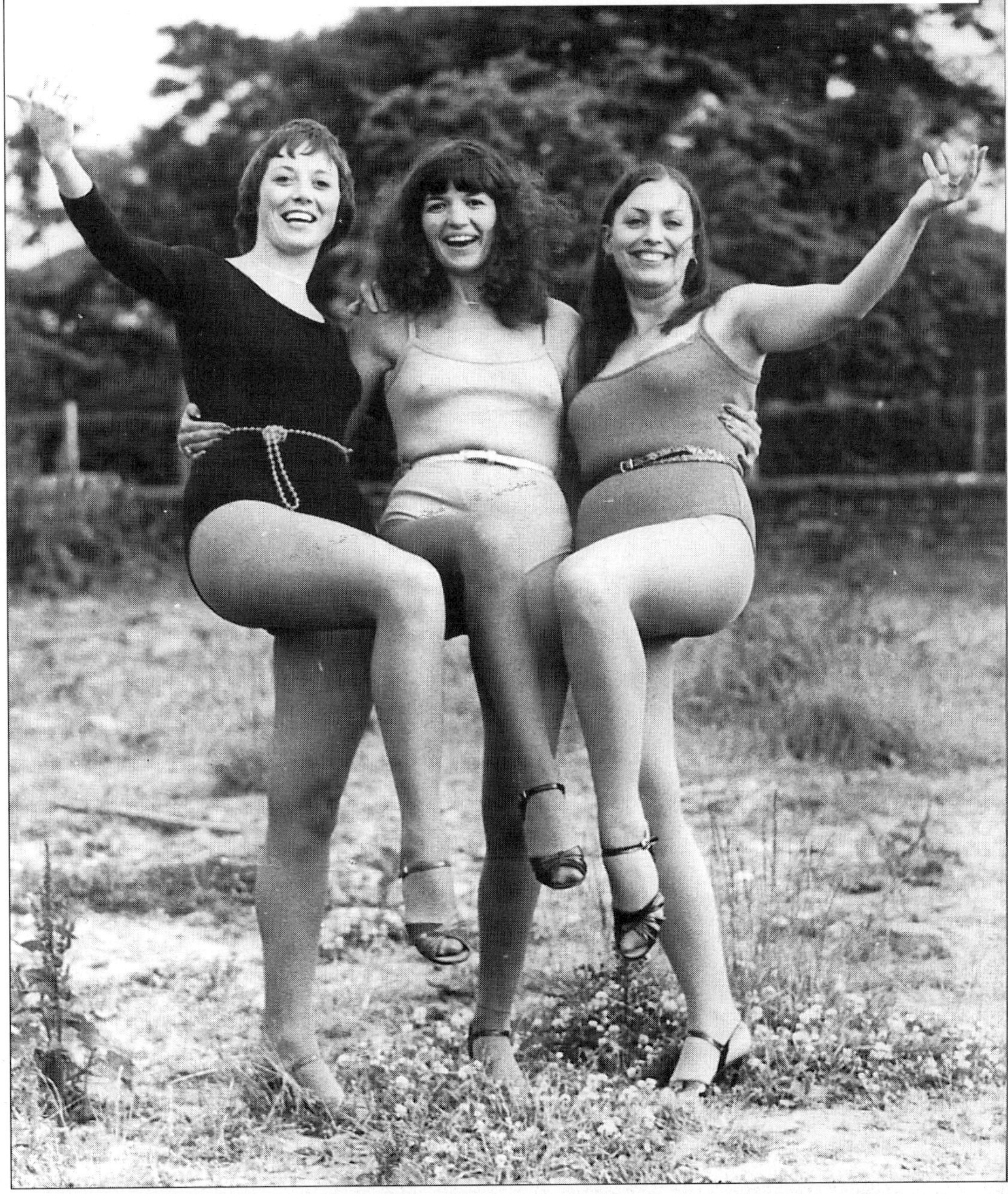

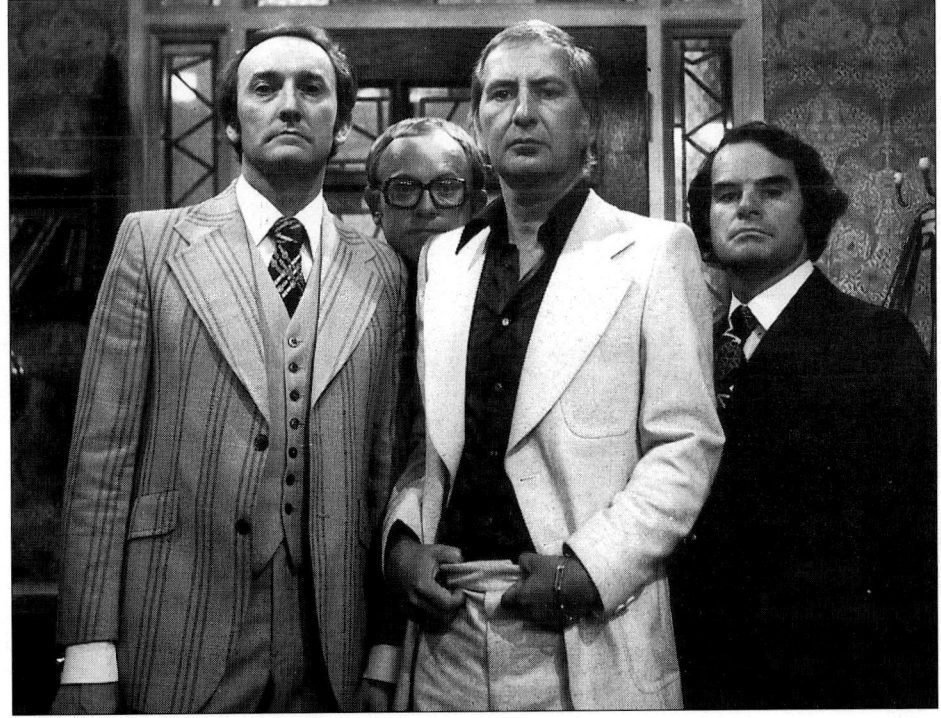

An episode of the ATV sit-com "A Soft Touch", 31st July 1978. The grim faced characters are Alton, Ken Morley (now a major star of "Coronation Street"), Paul McDowall (originally "The Man in the White Suit" with The Temperance Seven), and Johnny Dennis (Chairman of the Olde Tyme Music Hall at London's Players' Theatre).

Dudley's comic/eccentric dancer,
Billy Dainty, c. 1980.

BLACK COUNTRY SOCIETY
AUTUMN PROGRAMME, 1982

Wednesday, October 27th, at 8.00 p.m.
" ON THE AIR-AND OFF "
Personal view of broadcasting in the West Midlands
Speaker: To be announced
Saracen's Head, Stone Street, Dudley

Wednesday, November 24th, 1982 at 8.00 p.m.
" BLACK COUNTRY BRICKYARDS "
Speaker: John Cooksey
Brierley Hill Library, High Street, Brierley Hill

Saturday, November 6th, 1982
Visit to Abbeydale Industrial Hamlet and Kelane Island Museum of
Industry, Sheffield.
8.00 a.m. Flood Street, Car Park, Dudley
Fare appro. £3 plus museum entrance fees
Book at meetings or phone John Cooksey
CRADLEY HEATH 636758

Sunday, November 21st, 1982 at 2.45 p.m.
The Wurlitzer Organ at Dormston House played by B. Sharp
Ticket £1.25.   Tickets from L. HOLLIS, DUDLEY 53615

Wednesday, November 24th, 1982 at 8.00 p.m.
" BLACK COUNTRY BRICKYARDS "
Speaker: John Cooksey
Brierley Hill Library, High Street, Brierley Hill

December
CAROL SERVICE AND NINE LESSONS
Venue and date to be announced. Phone L. Hollis for details

Tuesday, January 18th, 1983 at 8.00 p.m.
EARLY CHEMICAL INDUSTRY AT OLDBURY
Speaker: J. E. HORNBY
Teachers' Centre, Church Bridge, Oldbury

Wednesday, February 16th, 1983 at 8.00 p.m.
OUR BLACK COUNTRY HERITAGE
Speaker: R. COCHRANE
Saracen's Head, Stone Street, Dudley

Wednesday, March 16th, 1983 at 8.00 p.m.
ANNUAL GENERAL MEETING
Royal Oak, Dudley Port

Saturday, March 26th, 1983 at 7.30 p.m.
A BOWLS NIGHT (including meal)
THE KINFARE RESTAURANT, HIGH STREET, KINVER
Cost about £3.00 per head
Telephone John Nicholls DUDLEY 211859 for details

An Olde Tyme Ball gets a happy reaction at its launch, Walsall Town Hall, 23rd July 1984.

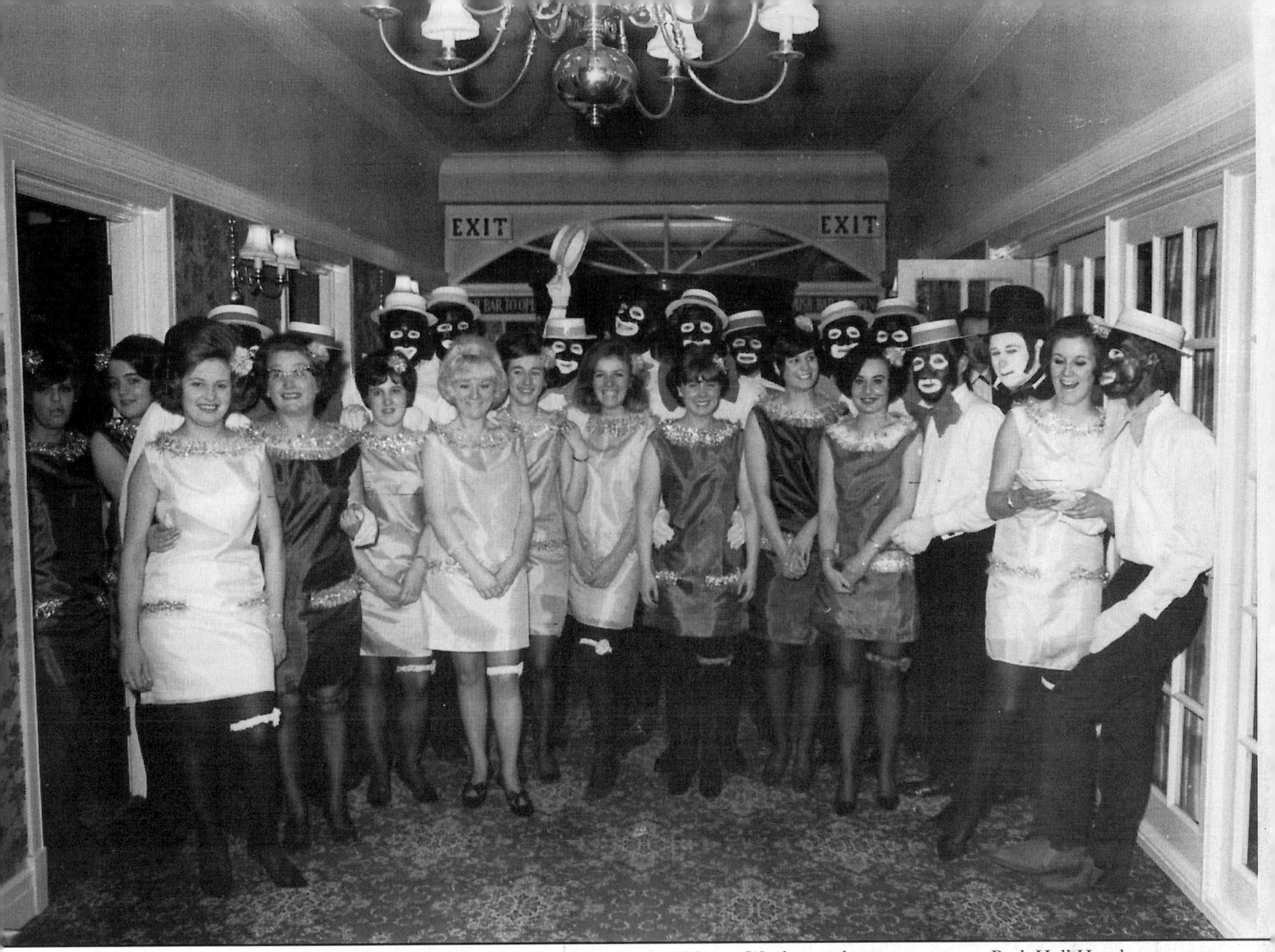

A Black and White Minstrel Show, comprising employees from Sankey Manor Works, ready to go on stage, Park Hall Hotel, Wolverhampton, Christmas 1984.

SAVOY
ABC
CANNON

1937
1987

CANNON
FILM CENTRE
GARRICK STREET
WOLVERHAMPTON

50th Anniversary
Celebration

Wolverhampton pop group, Slade, 26th May 1984.

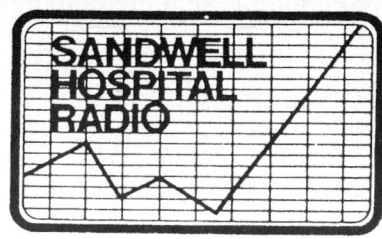

SANDWELL HOSPITAL RADIO
presents
THE

ALL OHIO STATE FAIR YOUTH CHOIR
- OHIO U.S.A.

in a concert sponsored by

WEST BROMWICH TOWN HALL
FRIDAY 6th JULY 1990

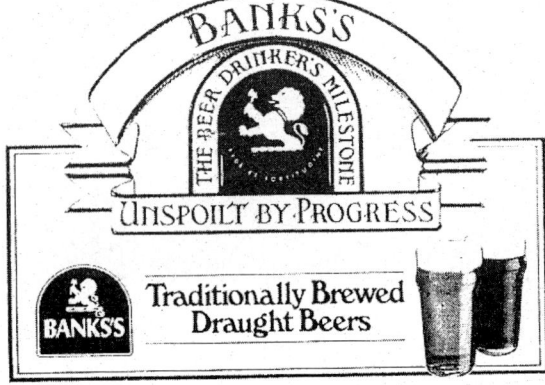
THE ALL OHIO STATE FAIR YOUTH CHOIR

At the beginning of July 1989, Sandwell Hospital Radio was very proud to be able to stage a concert in West Bromwich Town Hall, featuring the world famous All Ohio State Fair Youth Choir, (America's singing ambassadors of goodwill)

The full choir numbers some 300 voices, of which around 100 embark on a tour of Great Britain and Europe each Summer, performing concerts in aid of worthy charities. All the choir members are aged between 16 and 19, they all pay their own fares and travel expenses, and make no charge for the service they offer.

The compere for this wonderful evening of entertainment was local showbiz personality Mr. Alton Douglas, who also gave his services free of charge, and made a donation to Sandwell Hospital Radio, from the sale of his books during the interval.

The Concert was sponsored by Barclays Bank, West Bromwich, and was relayed live to hospitalised patients throughout the Borough of Sandwell, and via our colleagues at other hospital radio stations, to patients all over the United Kingdom.

The concert was a marvellous success, both financially (raising money towards the Sandwell Hospital Radio Editing Suite Appeal), and as an exercise in International relations. In addition the atmosphere at the Town Hall was absolutely electric.

The day following the concert, the Choir visited the Sandwell District General Hospital, and sang a few songs for patients-adding greatly to their already fine reputation.

We are delighted to be able to announce that on Friday 6th July 1990, the All Ohio State Fair Youth Choir will once again be performing in aid of Sandwell Hospital Radio at West Bromwich Town Hall. It really is an event not to be missed, and tickets are likely to sell-out very quickly - so book early!

Clive Reeves. Image Projection Officer.

Smethwick-born actress, Liza Goddard, with Eric-the-dog (played by Tich) in Central Independent Television's production of the children's programme "Woof", 1990.

Cabaret singer Lesley Ann Fuchs (stage name Vivi Caan) sings at her old school, Colton Hills, Wolverhampton, on 1st October 1992. She is accompanied by pupils Hester Fairclough (L) and Siobhan Cummins.

Andy Hamilton, Bear Tavern, Bearwood, 1993.

Jimmy Witherspoon, Bear Tavern, Bearwood, 16th March 1993.

Singer Chaka Khan at the Robin R "n" B Club, Robin Hood, Merry Hill, February 1994..

Josie Lawrence, actress and comedienne, was born in Old Hill and attended Rowley Regis Grammar School.

Dudley comedian and actor, Lenny Henry.

Penn Fields' Denis Beards ("Comedian - Almost a Magician").

![A jazz evening at the Wharf Bar](live at... THE WHARF)

A jazz evening at the Wharf Bar, Boundary Hotel, Birmingham Road, Walsall, March 1994.

Great Bridge actor, Raymond Mason, appears as "Svengali" in "Trilby", Chesterfield Repertory Company, 1955...

...and Raymond, as himself, today.

The Walsall Leather Museum, Wisemore.

Walsall Leather Festival Horse Parade, 1991.

The Mayor of Walsall, Coun. Alan Davis, arrives in style at the Museum, 1991.

Help with the harnessing, Walsall Leather Museum, 1991.

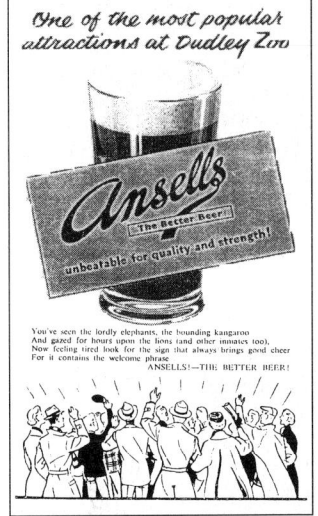
Comedy double act, Jimmy Jewel and Ben Warris, with bandleader Geraldo, help the popular vocalist, Sally Barnes, christen a zebra, Dudley Zoo, 31st July 1954.

Next please! Camel rides, Dudley Zoo, August Bank Holiday, 1957.

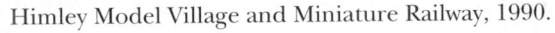

Himley Model Village and Miniature Railway, 1990.

Beacon Radio

97.2 FM (West Midlands)
103.1 FM (Shropshire)

Will Tudor

Ian Perry

Alan Nicklin

Niel Jackson

Stuart Hickman

Chuck

RADIO WABC

303 MW (West Midlands)
295 MW (Shropshire)

Dave Myatt

Dave Parkes

Tony Richards

Mike Wyer

Jason King

Jim Duncan

The Mayor of Sandwell, Coun. Jack Smith, receives a copy of "The Black Country at War" from Beacon Radio's then-managing Director, Peter Tomlinson and Alton, West Bromwich Town Hall, 5th November 1984.

ACKNOWLEDGEMENTS
(for providing photographs, for encouragement and numerous other favours)

Keith Berry; Anne Beverley; Bilston Operatic Company; Birmingham Post & Mail Ltd.; Nell Blackburn; Black Country Museum; Fred Blakemore; Jim Boulton; Brierley Hill Library; L.S. Canty Silkscreen & General Printer; Dave Carpenter; Central Independant Television plc; Civic Hall, Wolverhampton; Colton Hills School; David and Pauline Conway; Alan and Brenda Cronshaw; Curves & Co., West Bromwich; Wallace Davies; Dudley Local History Centre; Brian Fisher; Barbara Forrest; Charles Forrest; 481 (West Bromwich) Squadron ATC; Gala Leisure Centre, West Bromwich; Ben and Pam George; Ted Gibson; Reg Gower; Ron Gray; Halesowen Library; Halesowen News; Geoff Hawkins; Roy and Margaret Higgins; Himley Model Village and Miniature Railway; Colin Homer; John Hotchkiss; Paul Jervis; Alan and Jean Johnson; Ruth Johnson; Dave, Thelma and Tom Jones; Kings Cinema, West Bromwich; Steve Lingard-Jones; The Lock Museum, Willenhall; Raymond Mason; Tony Matthews; Niels McGuiness; Pat Mills; Walter Mott; Tommy Mundon; One-Stop Printshop; Martyn Parsons; Margaret Pennington; Brian and Winnie Price; Geoff and Linda Price; Roy Pumphrey; Queen Victoria Primary School, Sedgley; Jon Raven; Brian Roberts; Frank Rogers; Bill Sharrocks; Angela Smith; Edgar and Tan Smith; Norman and Jean Southall; Brian Steel; Chris Swaithes; Tipton Swimming and Fitness Centre; Anne Tomkinson; Brian Thompson (B.T. Supplies, Stourbridge); Brian and Jan Thompson; 240 (Darlaston) Squadron ATC; Uplands Junior School, Finchfield; Andy Wade; Walsall Council, Dept. of Community Services; Walsall Leather Museum; Joan Wanty; Warley Divers; West Bromwich Dartmouth CC; Keith White; Arthur Williams; Wolverhampton Company of Archers.

Please forgive any possible omissions. Every effort has been made to include all organisations and individuals involved in the book.

Back Cover: *Top:*   Aerobics class, Curves Dance Exercise Studio, High Street, West Bromwich, December 1992.

               Bottom: Geoff and Linda Price, of Wednesbury, with just part of their personal collection of model vehicles, 1991. They are also the organisers of several motoring events and toy collectors' fairs, under the banner of Transtar Promotions.